Button Reflections

Button Reflections

Patricia Budd Kepler

To order additional copies of this book, contact:
Xlibris
1-888-795-4274
www.Xlibris.com
Orders@Xlibris.com
553695

Contents

This book is dedicated to the members of the Westminster Presbyterian Church, once in Manalapan, New Jersey, those living on earth and those living in Glory. Theirs was the first church I served. They loved me into being a Minister and a better human being. To them I offer my deepest gratitude.

I also dedicate this book to my husband, Thomas Kepler, who opened the door for me at Manalapan. Through love and grace we stay life's course together.

We are grateful to all those with whom we have worked and whom we have cherished in other churches and other contexts. God is good!

INTRODUCTION

W HO KNEW THAT rummaging through a desk drawer could be an adventure? There among the pens, scotch tape, old cards, and paper clips were buttons. Not the kind you sew on clothes to hold them together but the kind with pins on the back that you wear to show some affiliation, support some cause, or just have some fun with.

As I looked at each button, images, events, memories, feelings, and perspectives flooded through my mind. I could see the people who wore them, the people I was with when I wore them. Endless hours spent in meetings in parades and marches, on fair grounds and city streets, scrolled through my mind in fast time. These buttons tell my stories, they are about our history.

I am not a person who normally wears buttons and I am not sure I wore all the buttons in this book. Some of them I helped design. Some of them I helped distribute. A few were given to me by friends or family. All I know is that what they represent has meaning for me.

Writing about these buttons was a challenge. I had decided to write no more than a few pages about each button or group of buttons. It was easy to keep my writing to a couple of pages for some of the buttons. Others are about issues such as Civil Rights or Peace or the Women's Movement. Books have been written, library shelves lined, movies produced about those subjects and the material will never be exhausted. I had to settle for being succinct and superficial. And subjective.

I found that in many ways, the buttons limited me. I had to stick with the messages the buttons tried to convey. If I were to write about my perspectives without the buttons, I would write from a completely different angle.

I also found myself wanting to talk about family members and friends as I reflected on the buttons and I sometimes succumbed to that temptation. I apologize for these very specific references. As you listen to my stories and reflections, I hope they trigger yours. And if you are young enough so that none of my stories remind you of anything in your experience, I hope you can find traces of the past in these pages that have some fertile thoughts for the future. Some themes keep repeating.

This book has been in the making for years. Life keeps interfering with its completion. By the time you are reading this, I will have stopped writing and stopped editing and settled for what is on the pages you are reading. It all feels incomplete. But the periods have to go somewhere.

I was amazed by how much of what I am writing about from the last half of the Twentieth Century is recycling again in the Twenty-First Century. My grandchildren's generation is grappling with many of the same issues we dealt with.

Each generation will have unique challenges to face, and the culture of each historic era will be particular. Our sons and their wives are part of a generation that learned to use the internet as young adults. They grew up without it. Their children, on the other hand, have never known life without the internet. In many ways, each generation is a transitional generation, living with new discoveries and situations.

The internet and newness aside, new years come and go, the political process churns on, human rights are still hard won, education continues to prepare us for life, sports continue to amuse, we still need food and water to survive, and being human means always adapting to change while some things remain reliably and inevitably constant. The earth is still our home. And we still struggle with war and peace. And I still read and preach from a Bible that is old and yet still relevant to my life, yielding ever new insights,.

So these buttons are part of an old story, and yet part of the ongoing story that belongs to all of us.

In the process of writing this book, I have found that many other people have buttons lying around too in their drawers and boxes. Maybe traveling with me through these chapters as I muse on my buttons will be an invitation to you to think about your buttons, old and new. I hope so.

My faith has been a central part of who I am, and is an integral part of my reflections. I do not often talk or write in religious terms. I see all of life as religious and religion as part of all of life. I have a strong proclivity for both mystery and common sense. Sometimes I see the Spirit at work in our lives and world and the way ahead seems clear, sometimes I know the Spirit is moving in ways that elude me and I move forward on faith. I assume the Spirit to be present and prodding in all of life even when I or any of us is not noticing.

You can assume, even when I am not using religious language, that I see the Holy or its absence in ordinary events and times as well as in special events and times.

There are many things that these buttons don't address. Most important among them is the family that was so vital and central to me while all else was going on. They are at the center of my heart. I only refer to them in a few places. Suffice it to say that my family made everything I did professionally, possible. And I like to think that much of what I did, I did in the hope of making the future better for them.

I regret that my experiences with my friends from Africa and Korea did not come with buttons attached. That story will have to wait for another day.

I am grateful for all of life, for that which these buttons has enabled me to talk about and all that was not included. For all of it, I give thanks. I am grateful for all those with whom I have been privileged to share and continue to share life's adventures, only a few of whom have been named. To God I offer my life, to Jesus I owe my worldview and my grateful heart, and to the Spirit I entrust the future of those whom I love so dearly.

Obviously, one of the most important parts of this book was gathering, sorting, and choosing buttons, and then capturing their images on paper. John Swisher, a professional photographer, is an elder in the First Presbyterian Church of Waltham. He is the person who photographed the buttons. Working with colored originals, he expertly converted them to black and white, arranged them and was patient with the process until the final manuscript was ready. I am very grateful for our collaboration. John decided not to read the manuscript before photographing the buttons. He is not responsible for the content of this book. Like other readers, he will be reading my words for the first time.

May Forkin, also from the Waltham Church, designed the cover with her skill and artistry in the midst of her busy life as a librarian and mother.

My husband, Tom, has shared in many of the stories and loved the people in this book along with me. We share a deep concern for justice and peace. I am also grateful to Cynthia Thompson who read an early version of my manuscript, and to the Rev. Catherine MacDonald who read one of the latest. My sons and grandchildren read chapters here and there and I treasure their perspectives. Conversations with them have helped refine some of my views. I thank Tim Tanigawa and Lauren Dvonch from the Waltham church community who commented on chapters, and my friend Betty Crosby who added edits to this book and has worked on many projects with me before this one. I appreciate Gary Martin's expert help at Xlibris in preparing this book for print. In the end, I am the only one responsible for the writing and the opinions expressed in the following chapters.

These buttons and my reflections are about both constancy and change. The last half of the Twentieth Century was a time of great shifts in American life. I begin with a chapter that reflects that constancy and change in the life of women in the Roman Catholic and Presbyterian Church, and in my cousin Sister Rosemary's life and my own. It also sheds a little light on the family history that helped shape her and me and my siblings.

BUFFALO 1991

DALLAS MERCYS

FIRST GENERAL ASSEMBLY · PHILADELPHIA 1789 · 201ST GENERAL ASSEMBLY · PHILADELPHIA 1989 · PRESBYTERIAN CHURCH (U.S.A.) ·

200
YEARS
CELEBRATE
THE JOURNEY
1789 - 1989

TWO RELIGIOUS CALLINGS

Dallas Mercys and Presbyterians

M OST OF THE buttons in this book are ones I have collected. I have chosen to begin with the button about the Dallas Mercys given to me by my first cousin, Sister Rosemary Budd. Tom and I were visiting her at the Mercy Center in Dallas, Pennsylvania and as I was telling her about writing this "Button Book," she reached into the drawer of the one dresser in her simply furnished room and pulled out the button you see. This button was among the very few possessions she has kept over the years. It represents many memories of a lifetime of ministry for her.

The Dallas Mercys button commemorates the Convocation in Buffalo, New York in 1991 that formed the Institute of the Sisters of Mercy of the Americas, bringing together Sisters of North, South, and Central America. Sister Rosemary was there on that special celebratory occasion.

*****

Sister Rosemary and I are the first in our respective families to have chosen a religious profession or as she might say, professed a religious calling:

she as a Sister of Mercy and I as a Presbyterian Minister. Her father, George Budd, and my dad, Harold Budd were brothers.

We share the same grandfather, George Budd Sr., and the same grandmother, Mary Shoemaker Budd. My great-grandfather on the Budd side, (Captain) Richard Budd, emigrated from Ireland with his family. During the Civil War, he organized a regiment. He was a lumberman by profession and the Budd brothers built shafts for the Pennsylvania coal mines.

The Budds were staunch Catholics. My father, Harold, was baptized in the Roman Catholic Church. His father died when he was about four, leaving his mother, Mary Budd, a widow with seven children to raise. Her background was Protestant and German. After her husband died she raised her children in the Methodist Church.

When my Uncle George, Rosemary's father, married, he married a Catholic woman, Sadie Meehan, and returned to Catholicism. My Dad also married a Catholic woman, Theresa Dick, a German immigrant who converted to Protestantism. When I was young they began to attend a Presbyterian Church, thus began my Presbyterian connection.

My mother's mother, who lived with us, emigrated from Germany a few years after my mother came to the States. She remained a devout Catholic throughout her life, attending church every day, and upon occasion, taking my sister and me to church with her. We loved lighting prayer candles.

Our family comes from both strong Catholic and Protestant traditions, traceable through generations.

I can't pretend that the religious differences in our family never caused hard feelings.

Grandmother Budd's bringing her children up as Protestants seems to have caused tension in the extended family. As my Protestant forebears tell it, the Budd brothers, who were executors of my Great grandfather's estate, (my grandfather died before his father) did not give my grandmother, a widow at the time, her inheritance even though she was specifically named in his will.

However, by the time Rosemary was ready for college, old hurts had been left in the past. She came to live with our family in order to attend Drexel Institute of Technology, now Drexel University in Philadelphia. I was still in grammar school.

During that time, Violet, Rosemary's sister and close companion, died of cancer at the age of 21. The family was devastated. Violet was gentle and beautiful and always remembered in faith. A picture of Violet had a prominent place among Rosemary's meager possessions.

It was after Violet's death that Rosemary became a Sister of Mercy. Before she entered the Convent, I remember going shopping with her and my mother at Wanamakers in Philadelphia, for some of the things she would need in preparation for her new calling.

I know very little about the next several years of her life. All that I know about that time came to me through stories handed down by others. I heard of her finishing her Novitiate and taking final vows. In the beginning of her ministry, she wore a full habit and took the name, Sister Mary Thaddeus. She could not visit her parents without the presence of another Sister. And when her parents went to visit her, they were not alone. She seemed to me to be far out of our reach.

Years later, Sister Mary Thaddeus reemerged as Sister Rosemary Budd. She had changed her name back to her birth name. She wore street clothes, and lived in an apartment with other sisters. When her mother fell ill, she was able to be with her and care for her by herself until she died. Later, when her father became ill, she was also able to be there for him.

Sister Rosemary professed her final vows in 1947 and I was licensed to preach in 1958. After being out of touch with each other for years, we found each other again in the new era, and I felt that we were able to share a special bond as women who had entered religious professions, albeit different ones. In recent years, as we aged, our connection seemed even closer and very precious to me though we only saw each other once or twice a year. Between visits we corresponded and deepened our spiritual bond.

One year, when my husband and I were visiting Sister Rosemary at the Sisters of Mercy Center in Dallas, Pa., she gave me a very brief history lesson about the Sisters of Mercy as she gave this button to me. I share the briefest outline with you.

*****

The Sisters of Mercy were founded by Catherine McAuley in Dublin Ireland in 1831. Her parents died when she was young and she inherited the family's wealth. She bought a house on Baggot Street which became the center for her early ministry.

Catherine McAuley had a vision of serving the poor and ministering in the fields of health and education. She took in homeless girls and women, and at one point even became the guardian of nine children connected to her own extended family of origin.

As time passed, other groups of women formed communities to serve the poor, following in the footsteps of Catherine McAuley. The Movement spread to New Zealand, Australia, and North America and then Central and South America and finally to other nations across the globe.

In 1991, the Institute of the Sisters of mercy of the Americas was formed. This is the event memorialized on the button you see,

*****

The Sisters of Mercy are a highly educated order. After graduating from Drexel, Sister Rosemary went on to get a Master's Degree in Business, and became Secretary Provincial in Dallas, PA and Secretary General in Bethesda, MD. Like other members in her community, she worked for many years in education, doing teaching and administrative work. Following the tenets of her order she was committed throughout her life to serving the poor and seeking justice for all in the name of Jesus Christ. In that service, she stayed abreast of the times. I read a note that said, "Throughout her life, Sr. Rosemary remained well-informed and her opinions were well respected."

Of great interest to me are the changes both Sister Rosemary and I have seen in religious life in our lifetime.

The Second Vatican Council (1962-65) brought about transformations in the Roman Catholic Church that are nothing short of miraculous when one considers the life of institutions and how hard it is to change them. The Council met at a propitious time in history and was guided and blessed with visionary leadership, inspired, believers say, by the Holy Spirit. The changes brought about by that Vatican Council were revolutionary, not least among which were changes in the orders of women religious.

There had been stirrings of new theological thought before the Vatican Council. Upheavals in religious orders had already begun as nuns engaged in higher education. But no one could have been prepared for all that would follow. And not all orders followed.

Change did not happen without the inevitable struggles that such change brings. Many hours of discernment, many difficult discussions, some divisions took place. But a Church which had been internally focused was now focused on the world and its ministry in it. The Church continued to stand beside the poor. Now it took on the structures of domination and oppression that lead to poverty. The Church denounced the idea of worldly economic hierarchies as God-given.

The Council also opened the door for enormous change in the life of Women Religious and the structures through which they served.

Sister Marie Augusta Neal documents that transition in her 1990 book, "From Nuns to Sisters," which ends with these words:

"A sense of challenge resides in the apostolic religious calling and the problems to be solved keep alive the hope of new reforms to come. The sisters are walking where there is no clear path. They continue to walk, in the light of the Gospel, to where God is—not only to where the cries of the poor, the suffering and the helpless call them, and to where those who cannot cry out are, but also to where the newly aware and organized poor reach out to take their place in shaping the future of the just society."

I was fortunate to have worked with Sister Marie Augusta Neale in the years that I was on the faculty of Harvard Divinity School. She was a great advocate for women in ministry in the Catholic Church and an unwavering advocate for the poor and marginalized, fostering the theology of "God's preferential option for the poor."

*****

While these things were going on in the Roman Catholic Church there was reformation activity going on in Protestantism. My denomination, the United Presbyterian Church (USA), was going through significant change.

The Presbyterian Church (USA) of today is a merger of the southern and northern streams of Presbyterianism. We are in the Reformed theological tradition. We are a denomination that functions as a representative democracy. The local church is governed by a Session, the regional church by Presbyteries, and from there elected officials make up the General Assembly where national policies and programs are set. Synods are intermediate bodies with primarily programmatic functions.

We were originally founded by John Calvin, theologian and lawyer, born in 1509 in Noyon, France. His primary ministry was in Geneva, Switzerland. He left the Catholic Church around 1530 and became a central figure in the Protestant Reformation, a founder of the "Reformed Tradition." Our motto in the Presbyterian Church is translated as found in the *Book of Order* in F-2.02, "The church reformed, always to be reformed."

The reforming part has been put into action over the years when the church has been called to speak on critical issues of the times. In the Fifties and Sixties, we were challenged to respond to the Civil Rights Movement, the Protest Movement against the war in Vietnam, the Peace Movement, and the Women's Movement. We were challenged to play leadership roles in these movements along with other denominations. It was exhilarating to be part of that process.

I experienced that reform in my personal life, when, after years of struggle, our Church finally voted to ordain women as clergy in 1957, We had thirty years earlier voted to ordain women as Deacons and Elders, leaders in a local church's nurturing and governing boards.

When I entered Seminary to study for the Ministry, women were not yet being ordained as clergy. When I graduated in 1958, ordination was possible for the first time in our history and I became one of our early pioneers, and Tom and I became the first clergy couple to graduate from Princeton Seminary.

It wasn't until 1974, when I was President of the Women's Coalition for the Third Century, a Bicentennial group, that I came face-to-face with all that these changes had truly meant for Rosemary and me. The Treasurer of

WC3C was Sister Concilia Moran, a Sister of Mercy and Secretary General of the order. She was on our Board representing the Leadership Conference of Women Religious.

The Board of the Coalition was meeting at the Mother House of the Sisters of Mercy in Bethesda, Maryland. One day as we were laying out plans for our participation in the Bicentennial and working on our "Declaration of Interdependence," I looked up and to my surprise -- there on the wall hung a picture of my cousin Rosemary in full habit.

It struck me, here we were, here I was, a Minister, sitting in the living/reception room, working and enjoying afternoon tea in the place where my cousin made her Novitiate; the place where she had greeted her family, years ago as a young Nun, now a seasoned Woman Religious in street clothes. My mind drifted between the past and the present. Here embodied was the face of revolutionary change.

Sister Concilia Moran made me a banner that says, "Sing to God a New Song." That is indeed what we were doing.

In that place, I was feeling a connection to Sister Rosemary's community. In that place I was grateful for the grace that change can bring. And there, in that place, we were women from all religious and political backgrounds working together and being welcomed by a close colleague and member of my cousin's Community. As we were drafting a document, "The Declaration of Interdependence," for our nation, we were living out its principles in ourselves.

*****

From the time of my first assignment as a pastor, serving Westminster Presbyterian Church, in Manalapan, New Jersey, up until the present day, I have had close connections with leaders in the Catholic Church. The priest across the street from our home in Englishtown participated in my ordination service. I worked with many Women Religious from all across the country when we were together addressing feminist issues in the church. When I was Director of Ministerial Studies at Harvard Divinity School, I worked with Catholic students and Sister Helen Wright, their Advisor. When I was pastor at Clarendon Hill Presbyterian Church, Pierre Auger, a Catholic was an integral part of our community along with his wife, Jill Auger, daughter of the Rev. Tom Fisher and Clara Jo, Seminary classmates, and Father Peter Casey and I produced a Cable TV show over a period of almost 10 years. And at Tufts, when I was Interim University Chaplain, I worked with Father David O'Leary, the Catholic Chaplain who later became University Chaplain.

I come by these Catholic- Protestant ties naturally. They are part of my heritage and, I think, a direct result of being grandchild of two beloved grandmothers from different traditions – and Sister Rosemary's first cousin.

I have lived to see the day when in the secular Northeast, if we are paying attention, old divisions take second place in the larger scheme of life. We are all Christians. We are in a world where interfaith issues are increasingly important. And we are in a world which is increasingly secular. We need to redefine our place. As I go about my ministry now, the old differences fade in importance as new ones emerge.

*****

I can't look at these buttons without remembering the strong sense of just love that the Sisters of Mercy bring to their calling. Or the strong stand for justice taken by the Presbyterian Church and other Protestant Churches. I say this well aware of the justice issues that still lie ahead and the works of compassion still called for. And the real stumbling blocks still needing to be overcome.

I am not naïve enough to think that our commitments to justice and grace are universally pursued by all of our members, or that those of us who pursue social justice have a corner on spiritual truth and practice. And I know that the wheels that reform theology and enact ethical reforms turn slowly.

I am aware that there are still important differences between Catholics and Protestants. For that matter, there are serious differences between Christians and Christians, Jews and Jews, Muslims and Muslims, Buddhists and Buddhists. And there are extremists in all faiths and philosophical traditions. These differences can even sometimes explode into violence.

My hope is in the God who shows no partiality. None of us have a right to believe that we are "it," the only ones with "the truth," who have it "right," God's chosen few.

One time when Tom and I were worshipping with Sister Rosemary at the Mercy Center in Dallas, Mass was being celebrated. I knew I was not, from an institutional perspective, supposed to take communion. Just as I was about to say, "no", the Sister who was serving the bread, put a piece in my hand. I, of course, prayerfully took it. Sometimes the grace of the Spirit works outside the limitations of our structures.

*****

Sister Rosemary Budd and I have each pursued our own callings and paths over the years. In our hearts we serve a common God and are guided by the life and words and works of Jesus Christ. Of course there are differences in our life styles and our church discipline, not to mention some theological differences. But, that which we share is more important than the differences:

we share a commitment to compassion and peace with justice. For this I never cease to give thanks.

When I last saw Rosemary, each of us, in our own way, knew that her days on earth were limited. We had witnessed significant changes in our lifetimes. New prophetic voices are being raised to embody God's Spirit in the world today. They will accomplish some unfinished agendas from the past and take up the new issues of the future.

The Sisters of Mercy have always been on the forefront of work with the poor and disenfranchised: that will not change. The stances of the wider Presbyterian Church have been prophetic, as have been those of the Methodist Church of my father's childhood. Freud was wrong about religion being an opiate of the people. Religion has been in the mix of those helping to set people free even if our cumbersome institutional systems are slow to change. There have been times, of course, when religious institutions have been actors in systems of oppression, or have been used by systems of oppression. Yet the kernel of hope in a better world for all lies deep within our religious communities.

My husband's family, unlike my own, has been Presbyterian through and through for generations. The Blains and Keplers have a long history of missionary work in China. I find that stabilizing at the same time that I find my mixed heritage enriching. And it is interesting that even with our different backgrounds, we hold so many values in common with Sister Rosemary.

Sister Rosemary died in 2013. At the end of the celebration of her life, a Sister gave me her Bible. It took my breath away, humbled me, and filled me with overflowing gratitude. The Word of God in written and lived form is the bond between us all.

*****

The back story of the relationship Rosemary and I and my siblings shared, was also a story of two brothers and their children.

Our family has always thought of Rosemary's father, George, as a saint. And that is because he was. No kinder, gentler, stronger, man endowed with a keen ethical sense and a twinkling sense of humor ever walked the earth. I feel sure of it! He lived all his life in a small town, set in rural America. In his later years he dug graves to provide income for his family. But he was rich in every spiritual and human way: a great man. His wife and partner, Aunt Sadie, was a quiet woman of faith.

My father was never thought of as a saint. He left the small town he grew up in to eventually become an urban lawyer and law professor. But in his own way, he was a man of God who was motivated by faith throughout his life. He was a man of courage and strong will: a dynamic teacher and strong leader and eloquent speaker, and active member of the church. He too was a spiritual man living life in the secular city. His wife and partner, Theresa, lived by faith each day of her life and was an inspiration to us.

Both men instilled faith and determination in their daughters, two cousins, both religious professionals, whose lives were as different from each others as were their father's lives. Rosemary was an only child after the death of her sister, Violet; I had three siblings, Mary, Theresa, and Harold, who have, each in their own way, proven that being a religious professional is not the only way to be faithful.

When I visited Sister Rosemary, I admired the simplicity and devotional discipline of her life and her communal setting. I look around me at my possessions and though I seek to simplify my life, I feel guilty. I have to come to terms with the fact that there are many paths to God. We are each faithful in our own way. We have each made choices that are right for us. We have each faced different challenges and temptations. We can learn from one another, but we can't be the other. So it is with all of us. All is well.

GRATZ AREA ANTIQUE MACHINERY ASSOCIATION, INC.
4th ANNUAL SHOW
JULY 20-21
1996
GRATZ, PA

8th ANNUAL SHOW
GRATZ AREA ANTIQUE MACHINERY
Est 1993
ASSOC. INC.
JULY 15-16, 2000

11th ANNUAL SHOW
GRATZ AREA ANTIQUE MACHINERY
Est 1993
ASSOC. INC.
JULY 19-20, 2003

15th ANNUAL SHOW
GRATZ AREA ANTIQUE MACHINERY
Est 1993
ASSOC. INC.
JULY 21-22, 2007

TRACTORS AND GREEN PASTURES

G RATZ, PENNSYLVANIA IS a town one mountain over from Williamstown, Pennsylvania where my father grew up. It sits in the midst of rich farm land, not tilled by agribusiness but by local farmers, many of whom are Amish. Looking out over the cornfields in that place fills me with a great sense of peace and freedom.

My brother Harold and sister-in-law Fran moved to Williamstown when they retired and shortly after that we bought the house next door to them where we spend time in the summers. We had a great time with them, enjoying laughter, fun and good food. Now that my brother is gone those times continue with Fran.

You can buy a house in Williamstown for the cost of a car. It feels good to return to the place where I spent many summers as a child even though it is not a prime vacation spot. We have many family gatherings there. We look forward each year to a visit from my sister Theresa and her husband Norb who travel from Texas. We also look forward to visits with my sister Mary and her husband Bill and their family who live nearby.

Each year, Tom and I visit the Gratz fairgrounds in July. One year we stumbled upon an Antique machinery show. This exposition on the buttons that we were given at the show will be short, as short as my knowledge about antique machinery and farming. Most of the antique equipment there is tractors. Rows and rows of them. There are also rows of more modern tractors, John Deere's in green.

Skirting the field of tractors are some antique cars. And in the center ring of the fairground where we have often seen horses run, are contests involving tractors. The day we got these buttons, the event in the ring while we were watching was a tractor pull.

I am not sure why I liked this show. When I was taking some vocational preference tests years ago, my interest in and aptitude for farming was off the chart…on the negative side. I suppose that means that, while my heart breathes in happiness in the presence of open spaces and fertile food producing land, I would not be any good at working on a farm. I didn't have to take a test to know that.

Fortunately, sister Mary and husband Bill, have an aptitude for farming. They have always had a small farm, and their home is a retreat where we can enjoy them and the fruits and vegetables of their labors and my sister's amazing baking.

So here my husband and I are, standing in the midst of rows of tractors of all kinds. We have just come from visiting my sister's family. I give thanks for her since I am not good at this farming business. Off by a storage shed sits an Amish buggy. I would not be good at being Amish either. I think Mary could be mostly at home with it.

I am reminded of the ancient connection we all have with the land, with nature, and I am clear about our dependence on it. Most of the Amish farmers in this valley still plow with animals and not mechanized equipment. Some probably do use tractors or have others use them on their land. In any event, here in the midst of these tractors, a city girl connects with something very basic that is important for our human survival: green pastures. I hear words from the 23rd Psalm where it says of the good Shepherd, "He makes me lie down in green pastures."

It isn't just the land and the open space that draws me into nature and away from the technology that speeds up my life most of the year and that is helping me write now. It is the way of life of the Amish and the other small farmers. The seasons dictate their work. The sun and rain are essential partners in growing crops. Some farmers irrigate but others depend on the weather for a good or difficult or even disastrous season.

Animals are their partners too. I have watched farmers plow the land with horses and work the fields with mules. They toil as one unit.

One day, as we were buying vegetables from a young man at an Amish farm stand, the team of eight horses attached to a wagon who had been waiting for him decided to take off. We watched as he bolted through the fields in hot pursuit. He did catch up with them. Meanwhile, a car dropped a young woman off to help complete our sale.

On Wednesdays we visit the antique flea market of our friend, Ruth Hoke who comes from a farming tradition.

On Fridays when we go to "The Sale," a vast farmer's market, their produce is sold along with clothing, sports cards, books, odds and ends, a whole host of things including large soft pretzels fresh from the oven (that we can never resist). The prices are right and the harvest is bountiful. Large baskets of almost everything imaginable fill the stalls.

We have a farmer's market in Arlington, Massachusetts, too. I am grateful for it but the higher prices reflect its urban location as does its contained size. But here we have fish.

*****

Antique tractors. I think about the word "antique." The word is interesting. It just means very old and almost always, well used. I am approaching antiquehood myself. And I think, is God an antique? People have worshipped God throughout history, way back into ancient times, times even before the advent of language. Are the mountains that surround these farms antique? Is the land antique? We are surrounded here by nature's antiques. Maybe that is why this place feels so good. Here one can feel continuity with the past as one stands in the present. Here one can imagine the future. I want the land and the mountains to stand into the future. I want new generations to be in touch with nature.

Whisper a prayer of thanksgiving for the harvest that comes from these farms and the machinery, however basic, that has helped produce that harvest over the years. And don't forget to whisper a prayer of thanksgiving for the farmers who till the land and the animals who are their partners. We are the benefactors of all those who like them put food on our tables. I am aware of mega farms and advanced technology. But here and on other farms like these is where we get back to the earth, the good earth we need to cherish and protect.

CELEBRATING THE NATIONAL GUARD IN WILLIAMSTOWN

T HE "131ST" on this button refers to the Army National Guard Transportation Unit stationed in Williamstown, PA.

I got this button when we were welcoming the 131st home to Williamstown after the first Gulf War. We spend Julys there and were welcoming our troops home, indeed a festive and joyful time. There was a parade on July 4th followed that evening with a ceremony in the high school athletic field complete with music, prayers and fireworks.

Imagine my Budd cousins and their families sitting out in front of our homes by the curb on lawn chairs watching the parade with the rest of the town. We are wearing matching T Shirts produced for the occasion that say "Operation Desert Storm."

After the parade and following party, Tom and I went to the evening event on the 4th with our cousin Betty Baddorf. Betty had taught some of the returning soldiers in high school, kindergarten or nursery school, and had special relationships with them. Most of Williamstown was there along with families from surrounding towns in the valley.

To be honest, Tom and I were not sure we wanted to attend the ceremony. We were afraid it would be a time of hyper-patriotism. I was thinking of another Fourth of July ceremony we had attended in New Jersey with the Rev. Charles Neff, a dear friend and mentor. After a rousing sermon by a colleague wearing a crisp white suit and shiny white shoes, Charlie leaned over and said, "He really made the eagle scream." But we didn't need to worry, that is not what this service turned out to be.

The program that July evening was a genuine celebration of our soldiers who had served in the Gulf. It was a time to express our commitment to freedom and democracy in the United States without turning nationalism into religion. It was a Fourth of July celebration, commemorating our Declaration of Independence as a nation. And it was a time for prayers for peace in the face of the horrors of war… a time to express our deepest longings for peace.

The Methodist minister at the time, the Rev. Elizabeth ("Pixie") Whitehouse, drafted and selected or wrote the worship part of the program. Her husband and two sons had served in the military and one son served in the first Iraq war. She had a pastoral and personal connection to the returning servicemen that more than qualified her for the task. We were so moved by the ceremony that I am including quotes from the prayers we said that night in the text.

Those prayers illustrate how a community can express gratitude for the service of soldiers while praying for peace; and at the same time, acknowledge the cost of war for all involved. After joining in a Litany of Praise and Thanksgiving for Deliverance and Comfort, we offered prayers for Peace and Healing.

Pastor: Loving Mind of God,
People: Heal the memories of our soul, and we shall live in peace.
Pastor: Eternal God,
People: Calm our fears of death, and we shall live in peace.
Pastor: Merciful God,
People: Heal the lands and peoples that have been wounded by wars. God, be with the nations of the Mideast that have been devastated with war; rebuild them with your mercy and justice. God, bless even our enemies, and we shall live in peace.
Pastor: Bountiful God,
People: Purify our wants and needs of worldly goods, and we shall be sons and daughters of peace. Ever shield us from selfish wants; may our crown of glory be pure and loving hearts that reflect and imitate the life of Christ, so that we might be called peace makers and children of God; and we shall live in peace. Amen

The whole ceremony that night felt right and profound.

Clearly, this service of worship reflected the Christian make-up of the small rural towns connected to the 131st National Guard Unit at that time. It spoke to the importance of faith in the people's lives. The service was ecumenical with participation from different Protestant denominations, Roman Catholics, and Eastern Orthodox communities. In a setting where the population is more diverse, the service would have been interfaith.

But in that valley in what was once the best anthracite coal region of Pennsylvania, if not the United States, the service was an expression of the communities it represented. They had seen sons and daughters, brothers and sisters, wives and husbands, fathers and mothers, sent off into harm's way. In the past, in the memory of many, this community had served the nation through working in the mines and had known the meaning of living in harm's way in a different sense. So many had lost lives in those mines.

Beyond the Service and the words, there was much inspiring, foot-tapping music and fantastic, exciting fireworks that lit up the night sky with their sparkle and brilliant colors. Welcome home! We are glad you are back! Celebratory expressions of the human spirit.

Now, years later, after more men and women have been deployed in the same region and more women and men and children have supported them at home, they are coping with the physical and mental aftermath of war. And on the other side, in Iraq, lives of soldiers and civilians have been turned upside down and lives have been lost and changed.

While the troops have been brought home from Iraq and Afghanistan, individuals and their families try to cope with the fall-out of war on all sides. Iraq and Afghanistan are embroiled in internal conflict and the threat of yet more terror looms large in the world. And ISIS (Islamic State of Iraq and Syria) emerges along with rogue violence of all kinds. Some American soldiers are back in the area on training missions.

*****

Welcoming these members of the National Guard home from duty set me to thinking about the Guard.

In a small town like Williamstown, in a fairly depressed area of the country, people often join the National Guard to serve their country and supplement their usually modest incomes. They are civilian soldiers, often with children and jobs they leave behind when they are deployed. One hopes and prays that their service will be on American soil but more and more these men and women are serving overseas.

National Guard troops were deployed in World War II, in the Vietnam War, in the Korean War, in the first Gulf War, and were also in Iraq and

Afghanistan where they made up about 28% of our fighting forces. This flies in the face of my general expectation that National Guard Troops will serve nationally, at home.

In the early years of the Gulf and Iraq Wars, Guard troops had not been as well trained or equipped for international service as those in full time military service. They were ill prepared for the tasks and dangers of a foreign war.

In my daily life in Arlington, Massachusetts, I am several degrees removed from our soldiers in action. In the Methodist Church where we worshipped until taking an Interim position in the Waltham Presbyterian Church, I knew of one member who is in the army. Others are veterans. I do know our Massachusetts National Guard is active overseas. I recently read an op-ed piece asking that our Guard be deployed at home and not overseas.

I read about the war and hear about the deaths of local military men and women on the news. But I am not mingling with many military families on a regular basis. In Pennsylvania, every Sunday that we attend the Methodist Church in Williamstown, we pray for service men and women who are overseas. For a small community, the numbers of people we pray for surprises me as I read their names in our Sunday Bulletin.

Many of them were in the 131st; a transportation unit that was on the front lines of operations in Iraq and Afghanistan, and therefore, targets for suicide bombers as they moved supplies across dangerous roads. Until the summer of 2011 there had not been fatalities among the 131st then a roadside bomb hit one of their vehicles and killed three soldiers.

It is not just the deaths and obvious casualties that matter. The aftermath of war is harsh. It leaves psychological and physical scars. And often it contributes to financial hardships as soldiers come back to civilian life in a time of high unemployment in already economically challenged areas.

In the Guard, soldiers are often older, married with families. And increasingly, more are women.

Many of the women and men serving in the military today are from lower income families in society. When they come home, they need all of the support a nation and its people can give them and their families as they return to civilian life.

I look at the button, "Operation Desert Storm." I love the way we name things. Did we start a war or were we just conducting operations in the desert?

*****

Today, I am more sensitive when I hear about the work of the National Guard on the home front, having become a little acquainted with their work overseas. I am aware when they are called in to prepare for and clean up after natural disasters, floods, hurricanes, and tornadoes. Recently they were called up in Massachusetts to help clear the streets of Boston after a record breaking series of snowstorms.

And they are called upon to keep the peace during civil unrest.

As I think about them, looking back, I have vivid memories of the Guard. For those of us old enough to remember, images of the National Guard employed at critical points in the history of Civil Rights in the United States, live in our minds.

In 1954, the Supreme Court had declared segregation in public schools illegal and the backlash was terrible.

The National Guard of Arkansas was called up by Governor Orval Faubus to keep nine black students from attending Central High School in Little Rock, Arkansas, in 1957. Then the Guard was federalized and they began to defend the nine to keep order in Little Rock.

I can see the National Guard activated in New Orleans to control angry white mobs after United States Marshalls escorted six year old Ruby Bridges in 1960 as she integrated a grammar school for whites only. I can still see the image created by Norman Rockwell of Ruby walking down what seems to be a forever path, toward a schoolroom door to study as an African-American child in an all white school. Her courage is palpable as is my fear for her. The Guard protected her.

The other image that comes to mind as I remember those Civil Rights days, is of an incident in May of 1970 when the Ohio Guard was called in to contain a student protest at Kent State. Someone fired live ammunition on students and tragically four students were killed and nine were wounded. No one knows exactly how or if an order was given for the Guard to fire.

The students at Kent State were protesting President Nixon's announcement that, as a result of the Vietnam War, troops were being sent in to Cambodia. Their protests against the widening Vietnam War were part of national protests that were gaining momentum. The death of those students was followed by increased student protests around the country.

As a result of Kent State, the Guard instituted a policy whereby they did not carry live ammunition into situations where unarmed protest was taking place. And after Kent State, the first official college course and program of study on Non-Violent Protest was launched.

Today we are seeing a return to the militarization of the Guard and of local police. They do carry live weapons and their use is again becoming an issue.

*****

Back to the 131st. Part of the celebration that took place in Williamstown when the troops came home after the First Gulf War, reminded all of us that the men and women who fight in a war are not the ones who initiate it. Whatever our feelings about a particular war, or about war itself, it is right to honor those who are sent to war.

We did not honor our Veterans in the midst of protesting the Vietnam War, some of whom were themselves at the heart of protests. We have learned a hard lesson and know that now we must give the men and women in uniform, returning from present day wars, and their families, the support they need. And recognition of the sacrifice involved in their serving.

One also hopes that we can be more astute about entering international combat; more astute about the propaganda we are fed. We have a right, in the spirit of American freedom, to ask questions. Why are we really getting into this war? Who stands to gain economically from it? What will the cost be in lives? How will this affect other long term financial programs and priorities? Is there a way to address whatever current international crisis that is before us in any way other than by going to war? How many civilians will die?

I look at the button again. Many memories. Much history. And still more history being made. I ponder. I believe I can be a pacifist and still believe in police action and the National Guard and the Military as a defensive protective force. That leads me to my peace buttons. But before that, buttons with words and thoughts

Question Authority
MINISTRY IS EVERYBODY'S BUSINESS
the meek are getting Ready
TRUST in GOD SHE will PROVIDE
IF ALL ELSE FAILS, LOWER YOUR STANDARDS
GOD LOVES US. JUST ASK HER

BUTTON THOUGHTS

THE NEXT FEW sections of the book are about the Movement years of the last half of the Twentieth Century. Some buttons were being passed around then that captured some basic sentiments of that era. I reflect on those sentiments as I look at the buttons. While they express common themes, everyone had and still has, their own interpretation of what those themes meant. What follows are some of my thoughts.

"Question Authority" At the heart of questioning authority was a desire to hold power responsible for its action and to lay bare the oppressive systems that held racism, classism, sexism and militarism in place. That power was used to functioning quite successfully under the public radar.

At its best, questioning authority, was intended to lead to greater equality for all in a world that was putting privilege above human rights and dignity, protecting stagnant and entitled structures. The military/industrial complex was being challenged for the injustices it upheld as local and national governmental authorities were being exposed for their racism. The institutional church came under scrutiny as well. Were these systems and those in authority in them, serving the good of the whole, of the societies in which they are entitled to function, or were they simply serving their own ends?

For some, questioning authority led to their feeling free and unencumbered by societal mores: defying laws that regulated drugs, experimenting with sexuality, exploring a variety of relational arrangements, and occasionally disrespecting property.

Often, those involved in seeking the greater good, also explored some of the more questionable expanding freedoms of the times. It was a heady period in history.

I find it interesting that even as the authority of religious bodies was being questioned, those bodies were doing their own questioning of secular authorities. They were prophets of their time. That did not prevent them from looking inward at their own injustices.

Eventually, for feminists in the church, questioning authority led to questioning the authoritarian, paternalistic, militaristic aspects of religions whose God was always male. The religious hierarchy which posited God as the power who sanctioned the human hierarchies which we viewed as unjust, was up for review. The hierarchal ladder we challenged went this way: nature was at the base along with non-human animals, then came women, next men, then God. And at every human level distinctions were made for race, class, and nationality. Simplistic but remarkably descriptive.

I remember many gathering of women when we worshipped and met in circles, deliberately and thoughtfully using the image of a circle as an empowering image, creating community and challenging linear authority.

For many of us, myself included, it was a time of finding our own voice, imagining a new human order that felt inspired by the Spirit, in dialogue with a God who was both with us and beyond us, more than the male stereotypes and limitations we had grown up with.

For those of us in religious community, our questioning of authority reflected our ethical understanding of God's will. God was a liberating God of peace and justice. From a Biblical perspective, we knew God as the ultimate and final questioner and judge of all human authorities, of all principalities and powers. God was questioning authority.

One of the contributions of liberal religious communities in the midst of the dialogue was their focus on process as well as end result. Jesus taught loving neighbor and loving enemy, forgiving, and, never seeking power for power's sake. In his lifetime, Jesus challenged the authority of both religious and secular men in power who saw themselves as beyond questioning. He was most revolutionary when he taught his followers to not fight violence with violence, or evil with more evil. And he tried to teach his disciples to not fight for the good with evil means, and to know the difference. Those who live by the sword will die by the sword.

Then as now, questioning authority and holding it accountable, ultimately did not lead to our rejection of all leadership. Though for a time, that was a temptation. Most of us came to recognize our human need for leaders, functional authorities with strong and fair moral compasses that were in constant need of being refreshed and restored...and reviewed by the people they serve.

"**Question Authority**." That button held reams of meaning. It still does.

*****

In the Movement years, grass roots participation was critical to the winning of human rights. The religious community's expression of this was "**Ministry is everybody's Business**".

Whatever interpretations religious communities accept for the role of clergy, the basic work of religious communities now and always, has lain in the hands of members. "**Ministry is Everybody's Business**," This concept fit in well with the concept of questioning authority. It implies responsibility and empowerment for everyone.

And where ministry is everyone's business, so is the theology that helps set the directions of ministry, speaks to the nature of God and humanity, to our relationship with God, and to our life together in community.

Ministry is no more and no less than living life in a way that enables us to practice the values we learn and hold through faith: people of good will, seeking to be agents of a more just, humane, and life giving society. This work, of course, is not just for the religiously committed or inclined, but for all who seek the common good.

Feeding the hungry, pursuing justice, seeking peace, engaging in healing, fostering reconciliation, comforting those who mourn, welcoming the stranger, loving enemies, loving others as self, sharing our faith, contributing to society through paid work and family work. The list goes on. Not a bad thought that this work belongs to all: **Ministry is Everyone's Business.**

Of course, the fact that ministry and theology is everyone's business, did not mean that no one should be paid to do ministry or that there is no room for professional clergy. As in health care, while taking care of one's health is everybody's business, we still need doctors.

As a clergy person, and as someone who has worked with people preparing for ministry, I believe that there is worth in our profession and value to society of an educated clergy of whatever stripe.

What the button "**Ministry is Everybody's Business**" was against was a clericalism that had crept into the church that tried to elevate clergy above laity in a penultimate way. The grass roots challenged that perspective. When some of us who were clergy wore symbols of office in walks and parades and in hospital corridors, we wore them as representatives of our communities, to announce that religious groups were present. Other clergy wore collars as symbols of office on a daily basis. Most of us were well aware of our place among the faithful.

Now look at the button, **"The Meek are Getting Ready."** What is that all about? This button was being passed around at a General Assembly of the Presbyterian Church in the 90s.

Being meek doesn't seem to resonate with the empowerment implied in "questioning authority" and "ministry is everybody's business," but the phrase, "getting ready" does. In fact, it almost sounds like a threat. I see it as a good humored promise and challenge.

This button refers to one of the Beatitudes spoken by Jesus, "Blessed are the meek for they shall inherit the earth." It is time, the button says, for common people to inherit the earth.

One could say that Americans are obsessed with the rich and famous. Too often Americans seem to be chasing riches and living vicariously through the wealthy. Who wants to be meek? The fact is that less than one percent of us live in mansions. And most of us are one job away from poverty.

This button encourages the majority to have self respect and appreciation for the drama of our own lives, to claim the earth as our own. We may feel that we don't seem to carry much weight in our society. But we are the ones who keep the wheels turning.

When Jesus said, "Blessed are the meek," I don't think he was encouraging low self esteem, deprecating humility and dependent insecurity. Jesus was, I believe, honoring ordinary people who are not puffed up in their own eyes or adored by strangers, and who live without the benefit of extraordinary wealth or power. He was saying that the earth belongs to them.

If we want a better world, the meek, as in those without high privilege, had better get ready to take their place among the co-creators with God in human society. The meek need not only get ready, they need to act. Not, of course, by giving up their status as ordinary people, but by elevating the sanctity of what it means to be a common person. All common people are special and unique in particular ways and interesting.

The meek don't need to take on the powerful with the weapons of the powerful. In fact, we can't. The meek have other gifts to use in the world: wisdom and imagination and determination and compassion and a vision of a just and peaceful world. Our voices, our votes, our taxes, and our labor.

Great leaders who understand this have contributed to the empowerment of citizens and to their economic, social, physical and spiritual well being for the good of all and the advancement of society. **The Meek are Getting Ready!**

Of course, as Americans, we are privileged in the world even if in our particular context we are poor or middle class. Acknowledging this, we can value, encourage and work with others for their own empowerment. We can see the worth in and learn from who they are. We can recognize that after poverty comes some form of being in the middle. Rags to riches is an illusion.

And now we come to the next button, **"If All Else Fails, Lower Your Standards."** I know this button flies in the face of some concepts of religious perfectionism and social activism. But I like it. It enables me to go on. And I think it is psychologically and ethically sound even if it is a bit facetious.

Lowering our standards doesn't have to mean, doing a terrible job of whatever it is we are doing. It can mean doing the best we can and not beating up on ourselves when we fail and have to try again, or make a correction in our course, or take a break when we are on the verge of burnout or just feel temporarily tired of it all.

Lowering our standards is recognition of our human limitations in the face of the enormity and difficulty of what we are called to do as agents of goodness and wholeness in our world. I appreciate the thought from the Newsletter of The International Association of Women Ministers. "All you can do is all you can do, and all you can do is enough." (January 2015)

I find another meaning in this button that I am not sure is intended. We are not holding the world on our shoulders or in our hearts alone. We are in this together with all those of good will.

There are times when we do have to act by ourselves, but more times when we have to join forces with others. There are also times when we let others do it. For myself, I have come to accept the fact that if something is worth doing, it needs doing, and sometimes that means passing that work on to others.

A corollary to that is, even if something seems worth doing, you may never know how your work or the work of others turns out. The end result of all you do may be even more amazing than you expect, or it may be unexpected, or it may never be known. Do it anyway.

Sometimes value lies in what you choose not to do. A wise spine surgeon once told me that some of his most important work was in helping certain people decide to not have spine surgery.

Of course, for the most part, in all forms of endeavor we aim to hold ourselves to high standards in whatever we do. That does not mean that there are not times when we step aside and loosen the reigns we hold on ourselves and others. There are times when we need to rest and play. Times when we need the freedom to experiment. " **If All Else Fails Lower Your Standards**." Or, at least adjust them.

The last buttons on the page say, **"Trust in God She will Provide**," and **"God loves us Just Ask Her."** These two are tongue in cheek buttons. One gets the point, "She" or "Her" for God. A more subtle point is in she being a provider. And a universal point, God, of whatever gender, loves us.

Obviously, the use of the feminine pronoun for God is a variation of God as male. It is a corrective statement. The buttons are saying that when we speak of God, if we need a pronoun, "she" is as appropriate as" he."

By extension, they are saying that men are not in the image of God and women in the image of men. (" So God created human kind in God's image." Gen. 1; 27a.) God is not masculine in perspective and action. If there is such a thing as masculinity and femininity, God is both and either or neither. Many implications are raised by taking on the structure behind the symbol of God as male and masculine.

Clearly restricting God to masculine language and metaphors limits God. Some have called it a form of idolatry. Of course, restricting God to feminine language and metaphor would be idolatrous too. But we had to try the feminine on for size. And, if truth be told it felt odd for many, so entrenched is the concept of God as male. God as female was even funny as in these buttons. It felt decidedly not, well, very Godlike. Not very filled with "authority" if you will. (to return to our first button.) And that was the problem. Women were not perceived, and most could not perceive themselves as ones having authority beyond the home. God with authority had to be male! Human women could be the soft side of God.

In the last analysis, the values and truths in the Bible, its inspired revelation, are not dependent on the patriarchal social structure of the times in which it was written. God is not male. But for some, it was easier to throw out faith than to wrestle with it.

Now, it sounds as if we are talking about an anthropomorphic God. We are naming God with human pronouns. We are using concepts that seem very human, "provide for" and "love." I think we are simply using concepts and images that we understand to speak of something/someone beyond our comprehension. Because we feel a deep connection, a relational connection to God, for some a Christ connection, we do speak of God using human terms. And that has meaning as long as we are in the flesh. We do know, I believe, that God is transcendent and mystery. We can and do also use less personal terms for the Holy like energy, wind, light, being.

Love, as it applies to God, is a human word which has universal and transcendent meaning. In many religious teachings, love or compassion, is a power that emanates from, even originates with God. One could say, is maintained and sustained by God. The greatest commandments are a call to love God completely and fully, and one another as we love ourselves. God is the source of love. We do not apply love as a human attribute to God, love is a divine attribute God gives us.

*****

As I see it, these old buttons still have relevance because ministry is everyone's business, we need to question authority, the grass roots need to rise and inherit the earth, and God is here and is coming in Spirit, neither male nor female and yet beyond all. And God is love.

The seeds of new theological perspectives have been sown. We have made major strides in understanding the Spirit's movement toward social justice through individuals and communal networks. It is up to each generation to notice the Spirit weaving together the parts of life that are life giving, joining the Spirit in gathering up the pieces of light that sparkle and shine with life and laying them on the altar of love.

Theologically, we have come a long way without dishonoring our roots and the saints who have come before us. Each in their own time embraced new revelations. We must be faithful to the paths that a living God opens up before us. Next generations will do the same.

STOP THE DRAFT

why do we kill people who kill people to show that killing people is wrong?

LET PEACE BEGIN WITH ME

PEACE NOT WAR

WHEN OUR SONS were young, my husband and I refused to buy them toy guns. We didn't want them to play war and we couldn't imagine their fighting in a war when they were just eighteen, eighteen and responsible enough to fight and possibly kill in a war but not trusted to drink alcohol! War itself seemed unthinkable. Maybe guns helped boys (or girls for that matter) deal with fear and anger and any aggressive impulses they might have, but we believed our sons could and would find other and better ways to cope and express such feelings.

I had grown up while World War II was waging. Our family like every other family around us was caught up in black out drills, rationing, recycling. My father served on the Selective Service Board. I knew all of the war songs. I used to march imaginary troops around the block with a pretend rifle on my shoulder.

I was not especially aware that my mother and grandmother, German immigrants were from a country with whom we were at war. I must have sensed something because I was reassured to hear the stories they told of how my German grandfather hated Hitler. Grandfather Xavier died just as he was about to immigrate. It wasn't until I was much older that I learned that he had served in the German army during World War I.

In many ways, World War II was glamorized. When our neighbor Jimmy Cursio was killed in the war, it was sobering. My mother put a wreath on his grave every year after that until her own death some fifty years later. I stopped playing war then. It had become real.

Years later when I found out that my friend, the Rev. Dr. Harold Viehman, had been a conscientious objector during World War II, I was surprised and reflective. Until then, I had not known anyone who was opposed to that war or even to war in general. His had been a courageous stance and I wish I had talked about it more with him.

I am not sure when I learned to dread war and became a pacifist myself. Perhaps it was the influence of my Presbyterian youth group and its leaders. Maybe it was common sense. All I know is that by the time our sons were born, I could not see war as a reasonable solution to anything. Certainly, I could not see it as a game.

By the time I was a young married woman, the Cold War with Russia was on. I became aware of the extremism to which some in our government had gone to track down "communists." The right wing was rabid. The President of our Seminary, the Rev. Dr. James Mackay, wrote a brilliant letter condemning McCarthyism, the most extreme governmental form of irrational fear leading to the pursuit and persecution of so-called "communists." Then came another "hot" war.

In 1963 when we entered the Vietnam War in a public way, our sons were very young. By the time it ended in 1975, they were old enough to register for the draft or to have registered as conscientious objectors, which one of them did. They were not yet draft age. War was becoming real and hitting home.

When the Vietnam War was being fought, resistance and peace movements were emerging. The country was fully engaged in protests and we, as a family, were sympathetic to the resistance. As a mother who was against the war, I was also concerned that young people were being radicalized in ways that, bordering on anti-government sentiments, left them vulnerable to other kinds of extremism and government crackdowns.

As a minister, I watched as young men from my African American congregation were drafted to serve. I supported those young men fully, and their mothers and fathers who lived day-by-day in fear. I was supporting both those who were against the war and those who were called to fight in it. It tore at my heart.

During these years there was a strong Stop the Draft movement. A friend and colleague, the Rev. William Yolton, gave leadership to this effort through his work with the United Presbyterian Church. Bill's father had been killed in World War ll. His office advised young men (women were not drafted) who objected to the war on religious grounds. See our **Stop the Draft** button. His daughter, Beth, a peace activist herself, gave me this button and participated in many protests. The draft eventually came to an end in 1973.

I became part of a campaign to boycott war toys and acquired my "**Boycott War Toys**" button. The opposition I had to my young sons playing with guns took on new meaning now that they were teen-agers. War was not a game. It was real. People were dying in Vietnam. And in civil wars in Central America.

The campaign did manage to get the toy doll, GI Joe, off the market, one small illustration of how effective the anti-war movement and citizens were. Mattel actually stopped making GI Joe for awhile. Sears refused to sell the toy. Later, GI Joe was transformed to be Joe, part of an Adventure Team to fight characters from outer space.

Today, GI Joe is back on the market, guns are everywhere, the National Rifle Association is powerful, and being against war has seemed, at times, almost unpatriotic. And owning guns, even carrying concealed weapons in some states, is growing in popularity for many, and is seen as a cherished right for some

At Waltham Day in 2014, our Presbyterian Church, Baptist Church, and Methodist Church of the South Side Church Coalition, had a booth that was a few booths down from the one at which toys were being sold. I was looking at some cool hats when my eyes lit on a stack of toy machine guns. I was horrified. A machine gun. I registered my concern with the vendor and was told that "boys will always play with guns and girls with dolls. Think nothing of it." Fortunately, there are people who are thinking about it.

Tom and I were sitting around the table that day with the Rev. Dr. Sylvia Johnson and the Rev. Dr. Imani-Sheila Newsome-Camara and some members of our churches. We were thinking about it. We agreed that we can't afford to see guns as toys and war as inevitable. Guns are a problem in America and war is a problem in the world. No children need to play with guns and both girls and boys can play with the same toys.

*****

Notice the button that says. "**Why do we kill people, who kill people, to show that killing people is wrong?**" Why do we? How can we?

I wonder, would Americans have accepted going to war with Iraq if our government had not lied about Al Qaeda being entrenched there? Would so many people have died? I ponder, are we as Americans capable of respecting a leader who is cautious about leading us into war? Must candidates for elected office be "hawks" in order to win? Are we becoming more susceptible to propaganda as our government and the media become increasingly adept at it?

Are we being numbed and distracted by all the silly celebrity talk we hear and see daily that mixes in with the news, as if such trivialities mattered? Or are we desensitized by all of the crime dramas on TV? Or frightened by the violence we see in the news?

War. Such a small word with such enormous consequences. My sons are now too old to be sent to war but my grandsons are not. And other sons and daughters and grandchildren are not. They all deserve to grow up and live productive lives. And they deserve to be safe in their neighborhoods. And the same applies to children the world over. Wars and guns do not keep us secure.

Yes, we need police at home to keep us safe, police who do not use excessive violence. And who practice their profession without prejudice. We need military men and women at home and abroad to enforce the law. But how? Those who choose to serve in the military deserve to be called into action to uphold the law, protect the lives of the citizens of our nation, respect the lives of other human beings, use as little force as possible. They should not be asked to put their lives in danger for the economic interests of a few. Or the greed and hatred of leaders. Or to maintain excessive levels of consumption. Or to satisfy the need for power of any nation.

One of the problems of our time is that we live in a global world and yet all of our military forces are national. I am grateful for the Peacekeeping Force of the UN but it does not reach far enough or receive enough support. We need global alliances, not just between allies, but between allies and so-called enemies, between nations large and small, for the protection of the lives of our citizens. So many children are impacted and starving all over the world because of war.

It is time to declare again that "We Ain't Gonna Study War No More." The stakes keep getting higher and higher. I think it is time to study peace again: in the populace and in the halls of power. How do we come to believe that all human life is precious and not disposable? When will we learn that we cannot obtain security with violence?

*****

We have something to learn from the thousands who resisted war during the latter half of the Twentieth Century. Much activity was local. I was fortunate to be part of two groups of lay leaders and clergy who came together in the greater Boston area to form the Interfaith Peace Network (IPN) and the Somerville Interfaith Group (SIG). IPN met regularly at the Clarendon Hill Presbyterian Church which was home to both a Presbyterian Church and a Mennonite Congregation. Mennonites have always been leaders in anti-war efforts.

There have always been religious communities, the American Friends (Quakers) along with the Mennonites, who have objected to war on conscientious religious grounds. In the late fifties and sixties, other religious communities were taking a stand against war. The national Presbyterian Church voted to support members registering as conscientious objectors and to see pacifism as a legitimate theological position within the Reformed tradition.

The official position of many mainline churches has been the "Just War Theory." That theory sees war as a last resort, waged in self-defense. And once begun, war is subject to principles such as limiting civilian casualties and treating prisoners of war fairly. Now those principles are being breached daily and are impossible to keep.

The rules governing war have been impossible to apply to modern war. War is not what it used to be (maybe never was). Civilians always get caught in the crossfire of war and pay the price for the destruction and death it causes. In modern war, citizens are on the front lines. They are the targets of war: whole groups of people are being targeted and wiped out. And where whole groups of people are not singled out for death, they are singled out for the destruction of the infrastructures that keep them alive. War creates refugees, poverty, psychological trauma, and physical suffering, death.

And now, we try to justify wars that are offensive and not defensive. Offensive wars entered into ostensibly to keep the peace and prevent war do neither in the long run. War to prevent war! That is unethical and untenable. The argument that we are keeping the peace and securing freedom through weapons of war is simply not true in the long run.

I remember the day that we decided it wasn't enough to have "Peace" on our pins. We had to specify, **On Earth Peace, not War**. Unbelievably, there were forces at work trying to claim that war is the way to peace. Is the bully on the block keeping peace? We found we also needed to make clear the need to join peace with justice for without justice there can be no real peace. Notice our **Just Peace** button.

Jesus said long ago, "Those who live by the sword will die by the sword." Today it is guns or bombs or machetes, or atomic or nuclear bombs. And now as well as then, not everyone who dies by the sword lives by the sword. Innocent lives hang in the balance, they pay the price for the actions of leaders or zealots.

In our peace work, many religious communities came together, each embracing ethics of peace in their own traditions and trying to address the new realities of modern war.

SIG and IPN had members from many religious communities, Catholic, Protestant, Jewish, Baha'i and Muslim. We met in different houses of worship.

Both worked to advance peacemaking, serve as a resource on justice issues, and foster cooperation in our communities.

There were many groups like ours across the United States. And there were groups of all kinds working to end war.

We not only addressed the wars that were being waged at that time, but the possibility in the world for nuclear war. We were a generation aware of the potential for world-wide destruction by nuclear arms. We had seen what the atomic bomb had done in Nagasaki and Hiroshima at the end of World War 11. Now we had nuclear weapons with even more deadly potential. We worked for a nuclear moratorium and wore buttons to that effect. See our **Nuclear Moratorium** Button.

Our Interfaith Peace Network and the Somerville Interfaith Group faded from the scene as leaders moved away and the national and social climate changed.

One issue continued to grow in importance and immediacy, the Israeli/Palestinian Crisis. We had touched on the issues involved in our local peace groups. Some of us now began to study this issue, moving eventually into a national arena with our concern. I will speak of this in the next chapter.

Locally and nationally, our peace groups had gone as far as they could by the 1980s. The country took a conservative turn. We still have secular peace and justice groups at work locally and nationally in the first quarter of the Twenty-First Century. I am very grateful for them. But the momentum is different now. A new groundswell for peace is needed. I wonder what shape tomorrow's peace movements will take.

We are in an era of guerilla warfare and rogue mass killings with the fear they breed. Lurking in the background are nuclear weapons All rational people should be terrorized enough by this violence and our potential for mass violence, to confront these threats with psychological intelligence, wise negotiating power, commitment to healing wounds, addressing poverty and illiteracy, promoting feminism, educating for peace, and being dedicated to and finding the wherewithal to enforce international law.

One thing is as certain as it has always been. When it comes to violence and its many expressions in the human community, we need to look inward as we look outward.

One of the pins says, **"Let Peace Begin with Me."** There is a song that repeats that refrain, "Let there be peace on earth, and let it begin with me." The older I get, the better I understand that principle and the more I long for that inner peace that is able to radiate out into the world. Peace-making in society inevitably calls for a deep and open-hearted journey inward.

Whatever our faith position is, it is in our hearts that we find the will to seek justice and pursue peace for the protection of life and the preservation of our spirits.

For myself, it is in the Holy that I find the peace that passes understanding, the knowledge that human idolatries are futile and dangerous, the courage I need to live life as consciously as I can, the groundedness to acknowledge human sin, and the hope to live in the light of love. And it is in meditation that I learn to quiet my mind and open my heart.

PALESTINE AND ISRAEL

O NE OF the international situations that draws us into the issue of war and peace and civil and human rights is The Occupation of the West Bank and Gaza by Israel.

After World War ll the United Nations gave Palestinian land, at the time held by England, for the formation of an Israeli State. Even before the war, Zionists had been actively trying to establish a homeland in Palestine.

Living in the United States in the aftermath of that War, many of us who had been unaware of the extent of the horror of the Holocaust against the Jews by the Nazis, and the murder of homosexuals, gypsies, and members of the Resistance, were reacting with disbelief and grief.

The United States poured money into Israel's development and became a critical ally of the State. While the alliance served to protect our interests in that part of the world, it also made a strong statement about our standing, as Americans, with the world's Jewish population.

Many of my generation were aware of the creation of the state of Israel but otherwise uninformed about affairs in that part of the worl d. We all heard about the leadership of Prime Minister Golda Meir, and were proud of her American roots. We believed the propaganda, "A land without a people for a people without a land." And I was amazed at how Israel "had made the desert bloom" into a modern nation.

I had had never even heard of Palestinians until the daughter of a friend came to church one day and told me she was engaged to a Palestinian. Slowly I learned about Palestinians, about their ancient culture, and their living in the land given to Israel. It was not a land without a people. The week after she came to worship with us, a couple from the Middle East came to church.

Munir Jirmaus was originally born in Jerusalem, Naila was born in Lebanon. They were both scientists and held doctorates from Tufts University. They had settled in the United States. Munir's family had been forced by early Zionists to flee their home, going first to Egypt and then to Lebanon. His grandfather was a Protestant Minister. Naila had Greek Orthodox roots. Fortunately for us, they became active members of Clarendon Hill Presbyterian Church.

As I listened to their stories and those of others, I learned more about that part of the world and my education began. Over time, our congregation took a leadership role in studying and speaking about the situation. Behind all of the propaganda was another reality. We made connections with the Christian community in Palestine that dated back to Jesus time and learned from the Rev. Fuad Bahnan, a Palestinian Christian with a parish in the US, that some Middle Eastern Christians had once come from Jewish families as did all of the first followers of Jesus. Fuad and Tom and I had attended Princeton Theological Seminary together. What we had not heard then, in the Fifties, we were hearing now in the Eighties.

We met Christian and Muslim Palestinians and Jewish and Arab Israelis living in our area. We were part of a task force formed by the Presbyterian Synod of the Northeast to explore the issues in the Middle East. We led conferences, inviting both Jewish, Muslim, and Christian leaders to speak. We heard from retired Ambassadors to the region.

Slowly the reality of the losses and suffering that Palestinians were facing was coming to light. Israel, in the search for land and security, was ghettoizing and mistreating the Palestinian population, three quarters of whom had lost their homes and everything in them. They had become refugees in the process of the establishing the state of Israel.

Over the course of its development as a new nation, Israel has made economic progress and found solid international support. However, they practiced and advanced illegal policies toward Palestinians that have consisted of continuing to bulldoze houses and olive groves, confiscating more land, placing ever more curbs on the movement and freedom of Palestinians, incarcerating thousands without trial, causing countless civilian deaths. Palestinians were living under an ever more aggressive military presence in desperate and dangerous economic straits as the Occupation ground on.

Through our relationships with Palestinians, we also learned about resilience and joy, celebration and dance. Underneath though, the pain of an oppressed people was palpable.

One day, I was asked if I would join a Presbyterian Synod group visiting Palestine/Israel, Jordan, Egypt, and Syria to better try to understand the situation. I did not really want to go. I always hated leaving my family behind to travel. I knew there was conflict in the area. I thought that if I asked the governing board of the church, the Session, if I should go, they would say, "no." Surely I was indispensible at home. To a person they said I should go.

The trip was amazing and life altering. We were shown the traditional Holy Sites with which I was not so much impressed. But I felt moved to be walking where Jesus had walked. I felt connected to the land of three great religions: the mountain where it is said Moses received the Commandments. The Dome of the Rock (built in 691 CE) where Muhammad was said to be taken up from earth. The Jordan river where Jesus was baptized.

I also found the experience heartbreaking. The Palestinian sector was quiet and suppressed while the Israeli sector teemed with life. I saw Palestinian children being picked up by Israeli police. It was a time when their bones were being broken as punishment for things they said, perhaps for throwing stones.

We were visiting Bethlehem one day and were surprised when an Israeli truck pulled up into the City square with a very large Christmas tree in its truck bed. Soldiers jumped out and set the tree up in the center. The Christians of Bethlehem had refused to put up a tree. They were not in a celebratory mood. Living under occupation was hard and demoralizing. And they couldn't even visit the Church of the Nativity as locals. Only outside tourists could go there. The soldiers had imported the tree to keep up appearances for Christian tourists, many sponsored by friends of Israel.

I was forced to reflect on all that was going on. The Palestinians had nothing to do with World War II, yet they were paying the price for what had happened in Europe during that time.

Over the course of its development as a new nation, Israel has practiced and advanced policies toward Palestinians that have violated their rights and their land. Occupation is brutal and I don't know how either Palestine or Israel can live with a constantly visible military presence, and the hatred cultivated by segregation.

I can still hear soldier's boots on cobblestones. I still remember a rifle pointed at me for taking a picture where they thought I shouldn't. What must it be like for those who live there every day? What is it like for Israeli mothers and fathers whose sons and daughters are conscripted? What is it like for Palestinian parents who fear for the life of their children every day?

It is hard to be in a place where fear and hatred are palpable and even nourished. Militarily, the Palestinians have no might. Israel is a nuclear power. (I remember when an Israeli, Mordechai Vanunu, revealed the reality of Israel's nuclear weaponry to the world, a reality Israel had denied. He was imprisoned for it.)

The Palestinian/Israeli situation remains unresolved as I write. The day-to-day living conditions of Palestinians are growing worse. Israeli Propaganda is stronger than ever.

Perhaps one of the most devastating practices that Israel has engaged in is collective punishment, a violation of international law. Collective punishment is the punishment of a whole people for the deeds of a member or a few members of that group.

An example of collective punishment would be the killing of 2,200 Gazans, the wounding of 6,000 more, and the destruction of the infrastructure in Gaza, including schools, hospitals, and UN outposts in response to the death of 13 Israelis. This happened in 2014 in response to the launching of rockets into Israel by the security arm of Hamas. It had happened before.

The infrastructure of Gaza has been destroyed and people are dying daily. Gaza is like a prison. Dr. Alice Rothschild, a Jewish doctor, while on a recent trip to Gaza, visiting Dr. Yasser Abu-Jamel blogs that people in Gaza have a continuous form of PTSD. Yasser says …"it can't be post traumatic stress disorder because it isn't yet post."The living conditions, if you can call them that in Gaza are dire. They require an immediate response from the world and a guarantee from Israel that "never again!"

Taking thousands of lives of another people for a few lives lost of one's own people sends a clear message that the lives of one's own people are more valuable than those of another people. Taking lives over and over again is inhumane and heartless. It is destructive racism.

Now, there is a Wall (security fence) that divides Israel and the Occupied Territories, usurping more Palestinian land. If it provides temporary security for Israel, it's long term effect ought to be clear. Doesn't it create a prison-like effect for Israel too?

My husband, Tom visited Israel/Palestine after the wall was built, 25 feet high in the area where he was staying. He and members of his group would visit the wall daily in disbelief.

Lip service is paid to forging a two-state solution. For this to happen, two states need to exist. They need to exist not as enemies, but as reasonable neighbors. The button you see is calling for **Peace Between Israelis and Palestinians**. That peace is becoming more and more elusive as more Palestinian lives are lost, more land confiscated, and simple living becomes more difficult as the occupation grinds on and Prime Minister Netanyahu, before his reelection in 2015, promises "No Palestinian State."

In the United States we are supporting the policies of right wing governments in Israel that continue to defy the no new settlement policies of our Presidents and our stated commitments to human rights.

I fear that, in the name of Security, the United States risks a right wing mentality at home as well as abroad as it colludes in these violations. Israel as a state could be a beacon of democracy. Right now it is not. It is an example of how fear and insecurity can lead to the use of excessive violence and the erosion of rights

It would be easy to step back from this issue as it has and can create tensions in Jewish-Christian relations. The relationship between the Jewish and Christian communities in the United States has been developed over time with care. Jews have suffered discrimination as a minority in predominantly Christian countries. They have suffered, not only in Europe but in the United States as well. Anti -Jewish sentiment still exists. America needs to speak out against all such expressions and to act swiftly against this discrimination. This does not, however, provide a reason to ignore the terrible situation of the Palestinian people and the scar it leaves on Israel.

Protecting our positive connection with the Jewish community has often required or been equated with uncritical support for Israel. Many Christian liberals have been unwilling to look at Israeli policies and practices honestly, for fear of jeopardizing relationships with neighboring Jewish friends and synagogues. And some conservative Christians with an end of the world prophetic view that includes the return of Jews to Israel, side with the state of Israel as a fulfillment of Divine prophesy. The religious landscape is complex.

Untangling these issues requires acknowledging the fact that unwavering support for current Israeli government practices against Palestinians, condones policies of the Israeli government that fly in the face of their own declared democratic principles and commitment to civil rights. Merging being Jewish with uncritical support for Israel ignores prophetic voices in the Jewish community and their strong history of advocating for justice on other fronts.

There are strong Jewish voices that have spoken and do speak out against the occupation and all that follows from it. The Jewish Voice for Peace is one such prophetic organization. They are vocal in their call for justice and peace. Their very support of Israel leads them to a deep desire to see Israel embrace Jewish values of justice that have given leadership to civil rights issues around the world.

Not everyone within Israel proper is Jewish. There are Israeli Palestinians (Israeli Arabs). They do not enjoy the same rights as Jewish Israelis and they also need to be able to speak out.

I long for the day when I can discuss these issues without being called anti-Semitic, more accurately, anti-Jewish, and without jeopardizing relationships with Jewish friends and colleagues.

Archbishop Desmund Tutu of South Africa, a Christian, who has lived through apartheid and seen it overcome, sees Israel as an apartheid society. He knows from his own experience that discrimination dehumanizes those who discriminate along with those who are oppressed. He speaks with courage and hope. He knows that with the right leadership, non-violent change is possible and there is hope.

The United States is not currently seen as contributing to a solution. Meanwhile, generations of Israeli and Palestinian children are living with violence and fear. If we do not take a stand for these children, the future is bleak. For their sakes, we must act. It is time for healing.

We need moderate yet passionate Jewish, Christian, and Muslim communities to advocate for peace with justice that holds all sides, all governments, all militias accountable for their crimes. We need a world that chooses life.

From what I know of prejudice, it feeds on propaganda and emotion. It lives on hatred and fear. It breeds violence and defies just law. We are all subject to its forces. We need to protect ourselves from propaganda and listen to, support, and protect those who preach and seek to practice peace while pursuing a just society.

A place anyone can begin to act for justice is in supporting the BDS (boycott, divestment, and sanctions) Movement. The BDS movement calls for us simply not to buy products made by companies that function in illegal Israeli settlements in Palestinian territory. You can Google BDSlist.org for a list of these. The Presbyterian Church, USA, the United Methodist Church and the United Church of Christ are among those organizations supporting BDS. You can find more information on their sites as well.

As I ponder these things, I think about the button that says, **Free Ben Weir.** It is from 1985. Ben Weir served as a Presbyterian missionary in Lebanon for 30 years before he was captured and held hostage by a radical Muslim group there. He has written a book about his captivity, "Hostage Bound, Hostage Free." In it he describes his conditions in captivity in Lebanon and his wife, Carol's attempt to have the United States pressure his captors for his freedom. He was eventually freed, returned to the States, and became Moderator of the Presbyterian General Assembly for a term.

Ben Weir's faith enabled him to withstand the terrors and tortures of captivity but it did not protect him from that captivity. Fortunately, his captors eventually let him go after some negotiations. This happened at the time of the Iran/Contra affair: Israel's selling American arms to Iran and that money being funneled to a movement to unseat the elected Sandinista government in Nicaragua, complicated and still mostly unknown by the public.

In 2014, hostages held by ISIS have not been so fortunate. They were murdered. The violence is increasingly brutal. The dangers are increasingly real for the world.

In addition to bringing the individuals who have murdered them to justice, and stemming the violence of the organizations which spawn them, we must put out the fires that breed them and tame our own propensity for violence. We need world leaders, with creativity, and heart, brave enough to deescalate violence and break its grasp on us. I want them to be on the ballot so we can vote for them. We need citizens who do not condone violence on anyone's part.

We need religions who speak out openly and clearly against their religious radical fringe. Moderate and liberal expressions of these Faiths are learning respect for other faiths and are seeking ways to live in harmony. This is a movement we need to foster. We can protect life together.

I can imagine religious faiths and secular governments which do not have direct investment in this area, acting as peace makers too. Holding all parties to account.

There are no easy answers. But it seems to me that there is an easy place to begin. An end to the Occupation.

A breakthrough in the conflict in the Middle East would be a signal to the world that there is hope for peace in other places.

THE
MOMENT
IS RIGHT
FOR IT

SANCTUARY
IN
SOMERVILLE

WE BELONG TO THE EARTH
EARTH DOES NOT BELONG TO US

WALK FOR HUNGER!
Sunday, May 5, 1996

COUNT
RESPECT
RESPEITO
TÔN TRỌNG
RISPETTO
RESPETO
RESPÈ
ON ME

CIVIL RIGHTS AND HUMAN RIGHTS

IN THE LAST half of the Twentieth Century, Civil Rights and Human Rights issues burst into religious and national consciousness with energy and urgency. My writing about these things briefly, as commentary on the buttons you see, is obviously only suggestive of the breadth and depth of the complex justice issues addressed in the last half of the Twentieth Century. These issues continue into the Twenty-first Century.

Early in my education I learned that in a democracy, it is the responsibility of the majority to protect the human rights of all, including minorities. What I did not learn about was the extent and pervasiveness of discrimination against minorities of all kinds in the United States.

When the Civil Rights Movement emerged in the early Fifties, I knew I was seeing democracy correcting itself, or rather, being corrected. On its heels came other liberation movements. Other minority voices were raised. Another wave of the women's movement emerged. And to an extent, homophobia and classism were addressed.

Underlying all injustices are the complexities of our human failure to value and if possible, love others as ourselves, our inclination to worship false gods, our unconscious fear of strangers, our capacity for hatred and violence, our beliefs that might makes right and wealth imparts value. And our need to feel powerful or related to power, at any cost.

Watching the movie, "Selma," released in 2014, I was horrified to be reminded of the sheer brutality racist white men in power exercised in order to stay in power and maintain racism. And the murderous rage of one white man who killed another white man for his challenging segregation.

I was also reminded of the amazing strength, sage determination, and fearless commitment of both leaders and activists in the struggle against segregation and racism.

This fierce struggle for justice on the home front, inevitably led many Americans to advocate for human rights in our nation's international relationships.

*****

When I entered the ministry in the early Sixties, it was as the white pastor of an African American congregation, Westminster Presbyterian Church in Manalapan, New Jersey, most often referred to simply as Manalapan. It was a time when the United States was being challenged to face racial segregation in earnest.

In our small area, we were trying to do our part to address the reality of racial segregation along with the rest of the nation. The force and violence of institutionalized racism was fast being unmasked.

The button with crossed hands speaks to the many ways black and white Americans joined together in the Civil Rights struggle. Once African Americans had begun and been active in the Movement and took leadership with determination and great courage, they were joined by whites who were dedicated to working to bring an end to racism. Young and old joined hands, thereby laying the groundwork for creating a better world for everyone. For many, it was a costly struggle.

The Movement itself was being led by men like the Rev. Martin Luther King Jr. and many other black leaders and activists who took daring, politically astute and perilous non-violent stands to end segregation in the south and racial discrimination in the north.

Images of advocates for civil rights marching, sitting at lunch counters, trying to register to vote, integrating schools, riding on buses, being brutalized by police and government officials and violated by ordinary citizens, are still vivid in my mind, etched in my memory. They attest to how virulent racial hatred was and how, even in the face of that, protesters maintained their dignity, determination, and non-violent stance.

As black and white joined together in the Civil Rights movement, wanting to join hands in the living of life in society, both black and white lives were changed and some lives were lost. One of those who lost his life in the struggle was an African American, James Chaney who was murdered along with two friends, Michael Schwerner and Andrew Goodman, white Jewish Americans. The murder of the three men by members of the Ku Klux Klan horrified the nation.

Their deaths were brought home to me when James Chaney's mother asked a dear friend of ours to conduct his memorial service, the Rev. William Hervey, a white Presbyterian minister from New Jersey. Chaney and Hervey had met in Mississippi and formed a close bond as they pressed for voting rights during that Freedom Summer.

Bill was the father of eight children. When asked why he would leave his wife and children to embark on such a dangerous trip as a freedom ride to Mississippi, Bill said, "I am doing this for my children. I want them to grow up in a better world, a world with racial equality."

The connection forged between Bill Hervey and James Chaney is a constant reminder for me of how individuals and communities of faith worked together during those years. In the midst of deadly racial hatred, many were committed to a dream of a democratic and safe America for all, whatever the color of their skin.

While the national struggle was going on, people all over the country were working at the local level to address racism. In my own life, I was experiencing the many ways in which black people faced discrimination in the north, and the ways in which people of good faith could work together to defy segregation and build community. I was also experiencing the force of resistance to those efforts and the pervasiveness of racism as minister to my African American congregation in central Jersey.

Members of the Manalapan Church took action to address that racism. They took a traveling dramatic educational program on racism that we had written, to mostly white neighboring churches. We established a Head Start program for black and white families from mixed income backgrounds. They started a basketball league. We had a dynamic summer Bible School.

When the Rev. Robert Beaman, a friend from Seminary, lost his pastorate over his stand on racial issues, we welcomed him and his wife, JoAnne into the community at Manalapan. Bob eventually became Associate Pastor. At one point, Monmouth Presbytery tried to shut Manalapan down by refusing to fund us. We managed to survive by eliminating Bob's salary and dividing my meager salary between us and cutting our church budget to the bone.

Members of the First Presbyterian Church of Englishtown, New Jersey, where my husband, Thomas Kepler was Pastor, of Old Tennent Church, where Charles Neff was Pastor, and of the First Presbyterian Church of East Brunswick, where Bill Hervey was pastor, worked with members of Manalapan in our preschool program, our tutoring program, and our summer Bible School. And they helped us renovate our building.

I celebrate all those who cared about racial justice and gave so much of themselves to support it. I am eternally grateful for their vision and hard work, their support and the joy they brought with them. At the heart of it all was our small, determined, committed African American congregation.

During those years, I was personally touched in a way that words cannot express, by the grace shown by the members of Manalapan, an African American Church, toward a young white woman preacher and her family when she was just beginning her ministry. That grace and miraculous acceptance paved the ground on which I walked into the future for a life of service in the church. They educated me. They loved me.

And they launched my career as a Pastor, who, when doors were just opening to women in ministry, was able to lay bold claim to my new profession. They showed me that mothers could work outside the home and in it at the same time. Because they accepted me, I could accept myself. As they worked so hard for their rights, I learned the meaning of strength and courage and hope.

Members of the Manalapan family felt like part of our family as our lives intersected in so many ways, in the church and around our kitchen table. Our three sons grew up with an extended family, members of a basically white church and members of a basically black church and a working mother and father. They were part of it all.

One of our members at Manalapan, the Rev. Elenora Giddings Ivory, went on to be a Presbyterian Minister and lifelong advocate for justice. She recently retired from work with the World Council of Churches. Her mother, Phoebe Giddings was an elder and one of the saints at Manalapan. She had a profound influence in my life. She was a strong and a natural leader who embraced equality and compassion as an integral part of her faith.

The struggle, waged nationally and locally, to end systemic racial discrimination eventually led to the establishment of more just laws for African Americans. The Civil Rights Movement of the Fifties and Sixties worked to eliminate many laws and practices that allowed blatant segregation in the south. And the Movement raised consciousness in the north about more subtle but devastating and pervasive forms of racism that could not be addressed by legislation.

Human hearts can and do change but that change cannot be forced. What we can do is make sure that acting on prejudice is not condoned by law, just laws are upheld, and excessive violence is not used by authorities against those seeking justice. What people believe in their hearts is what they believe in their hearts. They have to change that themselves, or not. We cannot legislate belief. We can limit acting on faith in ways that threaten the life and well being of others.

The button that says, "**The Time is right for It**" comes from the days of the Civil Rights Movement when some were advocating for change at a slower pace. Those who were moving on knew immediate action was needed. They recognized that lives were being harmed, a national resource, that of our African American citizens, was being lost, and a nation was finally addressing racism. Change for the better was in motion and had to stay in motion. The time is always right for changes that bring about and insure equality for all.

While we need to acknowledge how far we still have to go in addressing racial issues in America, it is important to recognize the many gains that were made during the Civil Rights years. It is incumbent upon us to honor and celebrate all those who gave so much of themselves to bring change about and who showed so much courage, dedication, and restraint in the struggle. And pay tribute to, and keep faith with those who lost their lives.

Who could have imagined in the Fifties and Sixties that we would have an African American President, President Barack Obama, who is the son of a white mother and an African, with a First Lady, Michelle Obama, who is African American? Unfortunately, we could have imagined the resistance he has experienced. Who can name the doors that have been opened for African Americans because of of the Civil Rights Movement?

Yet, in the United States today, racism is again rearing its head and black and white hands need to join to bring about justice.

In 2015, we have had to face the use of excessive police force against unarmed black men, the killing of Freddie Gray in Baltimore and the protests that followed being just one example. We were being called to address racial injustices in other forms when tragedy struck.

In June of 2015, we experienced the tragic mass murder of nine African Americans in Charleston, South Carolina during Bible Study in historic Emanuel African Methodist Episcopal Church. Among those shot was the Rev. Senator Clementa Pinkney, Pastor of the Church and a leading moral voice in government. The shooting was by a 21 year old with rampant racial hatred in his heart, white supremacy in his mind, and a gun in his hand. President Obama facing this, the fourth mass murder during his terms of office, saddened, mourning, and righteously angered, spoke out passionately for gun control and said that racism is in our American DNA.

Across the country, black and white alike, are devastated to be facing racial violence once again in America. The reality is that racism has been an undercurrent through the years. Racism may be embedded in us like DNA, but unlike DNA, it is not a given, it is a choice. Even if it were a given, it can be treated. We can and must choose to face prejudice head on. As a nation, we must make clear that we will not stand for it.

I believe we can celebrate the progress that has been made without denying how much work there is yet to do. All the dreams of those who led and participated in the Civil rights movement were not realized. There was tragedy then as well as now in the midst of achievement. Yet, all those who put their lives on the line made great strides and have left us with a powerful legacy and dreams and responsibilities to fulfill. Their work was not in vain. We can and must carry it on. And we must continue to expand the agenda.

Before he was assassinated, the Rev. Dr. King called our attention to the need to end the War in Vietnam and address issues of poverty in the United States. He knew that the causes of inequality are complex and that human rights are indivisible. The Civil Rights Movement awakened other justice initiatives.

Another button, **the tree with leaves of many colors,** speaks to the ongoing concerns and far ranging advocacy for justice that came out of the Civil Rights Movement. The long term agenda became the establishment of a nation in which all races can live peaceably together as people on a common tree of life. The tree of life for the healing of nations is a powerful and hopeful image from the New Testament. We are all branches and leaves of the same tree, rooted in a common humanity, and, some would say, I among them, in a God who shows no partiality.

During the civil rights era, the civil rights of Hispanic Americans, Asian Americans, and Native Americans rose to the fore. Among myriads of current issues, we became aware of the discrimination that many Asian Americans had faced in the building of our nation as they provided hard labor for railroads and other construction projects. Then, known as the "Yellow Peril" they were denied the right to become naturalized citizens because laws reserved that right for Europeans. We became aware of the discrimination Japanese Americans had faced during World War 11 with many being interred in camps. We faced again the plight of Native Americans forced to live on Reservations in the course of the founding of the United States. "The United States has entered into three hundred seventy-four treaties with the Indians and has broken every one." (researched by Thomas F. Kepler for the Interfaith Peace Network in 1992.)

One button says, **"We Belong to the Earth*Earth Does Not Belong to Us."** In many ways, the dispossession of land, and the decimation of culture that Native Americans experienced with the coming of Europeans to their world, is the longest standing blight on our history and it continues to the present day. Still we learn from them. In a day when we are becoming aware of a need to protect our planet, Native Americans' respect for the earth teaches a strong lesson.

We all need a secure place in the social fabric of our society where our heritage is valued. In this nation of immigrants, including early Europeans, and early African Americans, many of whom were brought here as slaves, Native Americans are the only ones who can claim to be native to these shores. The rest of us are all immigrants. We would do well to remember that.

As each new wave of immigrants has come, we have seen new struggles for acceptance and for a place in the ongoing dynamic formation of our nation.

*****

Somerville, Massachusetts, is, in many ways, a locality that has welcomed wave after wave of immigrants. I served there as the Pastor of Clarendon Hill Presbyterian Church, which was founded by immigrants from Nova Scotia. Another church with roots in Nova Scotia, Union Square Presbyterian, and then Trinity Italian Church had merged with them by the time I was called as Pastor. The merger occurred because a city that was once predominately Protestant became predominately Roman Catholic as waves of immigrants continued to come to Somerville. Our dear friend, the Rev. Dr. Allen Fairfax is now the Pastor there.

During my time as Pastor, people from the Middle East and Africa joined our church community, some because of the proximity of Tufts University. Emanuel Ekumah from Cameroon, Aboro Abebe from Ethiopia, and Francis Situma from Kenya who became like adopted family.

The city and its religious communities provides a study in miniature of the gifts that people from different nationalities and ethnic communities bring to society and the growth pains of a nation trying to welcome diversity as tide after tide of immigrants grace our shores.

Through the years, in addition to discrimination based on race or nationality, discrimination based on religion was alive and well. Freedom of religion, a hard-fought-for American right, is not always easy to practice. Protestant groups discriminated against other Protestant groups, Protestants and Roman Catholics against each other, Christians against Jews. And, in more recent times, Muslims have come under attack. In the face of this reality, Interfaith Networks were formed to help bring religious communities together for cooperation and support.

The buttons that say **Count on Me** came out of Somerville's determination to create a city that is inclusive and vibrant. And it came as the result of some of the conflict created by diversity.

In the 1990's violence among youth broke out in the Somerville High School and surrounding communities. Questions were raised about whether this was ethnic gang violence or racism, or the result of cutbacks in service and unemployment among youth.

Amid the tensions that were on the rise locally, our country was engaged in conflicts in Central America. Were these conflicts at play among young people locally?

This focus settled specifically on people from Nicaragua, Guatemala and finally El Salvador where civil wars were raging against dictatorial governments. The United States seemed to be standing with right wing governments accused of the murder of civilians and the wiping out of whole ethnic villages. Our government justified these allegiances by saying that those challenging these governments were leftist leaning.

During this time Liberation Theology became a force for human rights and religious leaders who defended peoples seeking relief from economic and political violence found their lives in danger. Some were murdered.

Thousands of refugees fled for their lives, many to the United States. The United States government under President Ronald Reagan refused to extend protected status to them through political asylum. A move was made to deport immigrants who had fled these countries, sending them into certain danger and often, death. Thus, the **Sanctuary Movement** was begun. Churches offered sanctuary and protection to refugees and cities offered sanctuary as well, refusing to turn illegal immigrants over to the government in an attempt to save lives.

Amid the chaos that was stirring nationally, the residents of Somerville took action. In February of 1992, they began the "**Count on Me**" Campaign. That campaign was an effort to call all citizens of the community to accept responsibility for making Somerville a decent and safe place for all residents regardless of race, ethnic origin, or immigration status.

The Campaign was a call to action, a call for all to respect the rights of others, to eschew violence as a means of settling disputes, and to defend the human and civil rights of all. And hopefully, to send a message about peaceful co-existence to the youth of the city. The Somerville Interfaith Network was an active supporter of the campaign.

The "**Count on Me**" Campaign reflected in buttons in many languages did not immediately end racial violence and tension. It did lead to the creation of a Civil Rights Commission and the establishment of Somerville as a Sanctuary City.

Civil rights and human rights matter at home and abroad and are connected. My own experience and religious commitment leads me to believe that God calls us, guides us, pulls us toward justice and peace at home and around the world.

*****

Closing this section, I must note that there is one minority group that does not need protection, the 1 Percent of the wealthiest Americans. As I write this, the Occupy Movement which spoke of themselves as representing "The 99 Percent," advocating for economic justice, is history. But their cause is with us. The middle class and poorest classes are in need of protection against the policies that shelter and advance the "One Percent Minority." Economic issues related to rights in employment, health care and social security are on the table and will be for years in the future. It is time for "The Ninety-nine Percent" to work for their own welfare and address classism as we continue to pursue the human right to life of all.

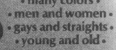

WE ARE
A CHURCH OF:
• many colors •
• men and women •
• gays and straights •
• young and old •
ALL SERVING GOD
AND SEEKING
MORE LIGHT

Tufts
UNIVERSITY

Straight But
Not Narrow

LESBIAN, GAY, BISEXUAL, TRANSGENDER JUSTICE

A S I CLOSE this section on human rights, I turn my attention to buttons that relate to lesbian, gay, bisexual, and transgender rights. **The Presbyterian Symbol in a pink triangle** refers to our struggle for these rights in the Presbyterian Church. This issue is last, not because it is of least importance, but because it has been the most recent issue to find some semblance of justice.

LGBT rights are about sexual expression and sexual identity, issues that in former generations, people didn't feel comfortable talking much about. Too often, it was said that the world is engaged in more important and more significant matters. Meanwhile, gay people have been discriminated against, abused, even murdered. They were not able to be open about their sexuality and many lived with depression and fear. Transgender people were isolated and their lives were often in danger, some attempted and some committed suicide..

The human rights struggle of LGBT people has been going on for a long time and is now taking on an urgency that is moving us forward toward enacting and enforcing laws and practices that provide justice in all aspects of public and religious life. And public opinion is shifting, though we still have a long way to go.

During the Women's Movement years, there were active and prophetic lesbian women who were "out" and strong advocates for their rights. Those were the days when it was hard, even dangerous for gays and lesbians to be out of the closet. The right to be open and negotiate family relationships and responses in the wider community, including the workplace, was happening slowly over time.

I was pastor to some parishioners who did not see a need to be openly gay or lesbian, to those who knew it would be a family or professional problem if they were out, and to those who decided to be open about their sexual orientation. I was also the pastor and friend to parents and relatives of lesbian and gay family members, and heterosexual spouses with lesbian or gay partners.

When the AIDS epidemic broke out, affecting the gay community disproportionately, new pastoral needs emerged and churches responded with healing services and ministries. Those were difficult and tragic times when partners and families lost their deeply cherished loved ones.

In the early years when conversations about sexual orientation were taking place, many saw orientation as a choice. Over time, it became clear that for most people, it was a biological given.

This information does not automatically change prejudice as people of color can attest, or the need to continue to press for justice. It did show up efforts to convert homosexuals to heterosexuality as ludicrous, inhumane and destructive. For some, it changed the ethical conversation.

Individuals and families were working through LGBT issues, many acting as advocates, as society was moving toward greater understanding. In the church, two main issues were before us: the ordination of homosexuals and same-sex marriage.

For years the Presbyterian Church, USA would not ordain open and practicing gay and lesbian Christians. And for years, small groups met in Presbyteries all over the country, including Boston Presbytery, to work on getting that policy changed. We believed that for people of faith, it was a simple matter. God loves everyone whatever their sexual orientation or identity. We are called to love one another with that love. And love includes, requires, pursuing and practicing justice.

Finally, in 2011, the Presbyterian Church (USA) voted to approve the ordination of homosexuals as both elders and clergy. According to Presbyterian polity the final approval of ordination for all clergy rests with the Presbytery and of all ruling elders rests with the local church. However, now, at all levels, discrimination cannot be practiced on the basis of sexual orientation...at least openly.

When I was serving as Pastor in a church in the Seventies, we engaged in a process of discernment of our own while the national church was wrestling with the issue. We sought to understand issues of sexuality and faith as they apply to all of us. As part of the process, we were helped by the witness to us of the Rev. Janie Spahr, a Presbyterian Minister and a lesbian. As she shared her story and that of many others, she enabled us to think about our own lives, attitudes, and ethics. For weeks we engaged in study. We focused on the sanctity of all life, the importance of justice in relationships, and the centrality of hospitality in Christ's church. I mention this because it was important for us to talk more freely about changing sexual mores across the spectrum of sexual orientations.

After this time of discernment and discussion about human sexuality and Christian ethics, we became a More Light congregation, which is a term for a local Presbyterian church which welcomes people of all sexual orientations and identities. We were joining a host of other congregations who were becoming More Light.

See the button, **Straight but not Narrow**. Homosexuals and heterosexuals were in this struggle for dignity, justice, and human rights together. This is a button I got at Tufts that applies in the church and in society as well.

While the church was wrestling with LGBT issues, more rights were being won for the gay and lesbian community in secular society. A growing number of States were and are declaring same sex marriage as legal.

In Massachusetts, same sex marriage became legal in 2004. The first day that it was legal, I officiated at the marriage ceremony of two women who were dear friends of ours. We knew their families who were delighted that they could finally marry. I was honored when they asked me to officiate for them. They had already made a home together for thirteen years and were parenting three children.

A colleague, the Rev. Jean Southard, also performed the marriage of a same-sex couple as did other clergy I know. In Jean's case, a court case within our Presbyterian system ensued with mixed results. She maintained her church position while the Presbyterian church maintained its stance forbidding clergy to perform same-sex marriages, until of course that changed, and change was on its way.

When clergy witness marriages, we act on behalf of the state and the church. And it is the state that legalizes marriage. We were acting within the law and in accordance with our religious conscience. I rejoice that church law and secular law are now in sync.

Finally in 2014-15, the right of same sex couples to be married in and by the church was approved and written into law by the Presbyterian Church (USA).

We celebrated! In Boston Presbytery, those of us who had met in homes and in churches to work for the full inclusion of LGBT folks in our communities of faith, offered prayers of thanksgiving as emails and phone calls flew back and forth.

Sadly some churches decided to leave the Presbyterian Church (USA) over this issue and join a more conservative Presbyterian denomination. This was and continues to be a major issue for many in the conservative arm of the church who see marriage between one man and one woman as a basic tenet of Creation.

I think that the right of LGBT people to marry has been so controversial partly because it challenges patriarchal marriage that makes men head of the house. This structure has been basic in almost all of our religious traditions, certainly the ones I know best, Judaism, Christianity, and Islam.

There is no doubt in my mind, that the acceptance of the marriage of same-sex couples does require some reorientation of how heterosexuals think about sexuality and sexual identity, and how we view relationships between women and men in marriage. I think it invites us to explore more responsible and ethical sexual practices across the board, as patterns of male dominance and female submission in marriage yield to patterns of equality.

Sexuality is a very loaded issue, shorthand for many other beliefs and practices…and feelings. Marriage between women and men has been the foundation on which the family is built. The acceptance of same sex marriage does not change this, it simply adds new dimensions. It opens doors that have been shut for same sex couples to the rights, privileges and responsibilities of marriage, and expands our understanding of family. We want love with justice to be at the center.

In many ways, conservative society has put the burden for maintaining the family on the simple morality of marriage between one man and one woman. The LGBT community and allies, in pressing for same sex marriage, has been pressing almost automatically for a deeper understanding of marriage and the family.

It is my hope that as a church, we are on our way to moving beyond surface morality regarding marriage and the family, to a better understanding of ourselves as relational people in need of knowing ourselves and one another in greater depth. I see us aspiring to a more mature understanding of commitment in egalitarian relationships.

Many ethnic and racial congregations have had a tendency to be traditional when it comes to sexuality and marriage, especially those who are new to America. They bring with them the perspectives of their native cultures. And some bring a perception of homosexuality from societies where being gay is illegal and dangerous and and misinformation is rampant.

For some who would not accept discrimination on the basis of race or nationality, or even gender, sexual orientation and identity hits a nerve and engenders fears that need to be addressed.

Seeking justice for themselves ought to inspire communities to seek justice for others. Yet, issues of sexuality are especially difficult because they trigger so many feelings about one's own sexuality, feelings that often lie beneath the surface. And questions of morality. There are Biblical arguments too, but these have already been overcome when it comes to race and gender.

In spite of this, Ireland surprised the world by legalizing same-sex marriage. Times and societies change.

By accepting same-sex marriage, society is not being opened for sexual immorality as some claim; it is being opened for more conscious sexual morality for all of us. Heterosexuals and homosexuals are equally capable of sexual behavior that enhances life or behavior that demeans it.

The issues that transgender people face are akin to and yet different from the issues that homosexuals or bisexuals face in society. For them, sexual identity and not sexual orientation is important. They face discrimination because of their chosen sexual identity, an issue most of us take for granted. Some people find a dysplasia between their sense of gender identity and the gender of their bodies. Finding harmony for them is essential to their well being and to life itself.

Some people who are born as women identify as men. And vice-versa. They need to change their gender to find peace within. They need to find recognition for their new identity in society. It is their right.

Many people have lost their lives over the issues of their gender identity. Discernment is often complex and difficult. Transitional surgery and treatment is expensive. Issues of acceptance and a secure place in society loom large.

Their situation is complicated by the fact that we may never be able to define what it means to be male or female. We don't need to. What transgender people are responding to is an experience of maleness and femaleness that is personal and particular to them.

My own perspective, coming from my experience in the women's movement, is that the sexes are closer together than we are prepared to acknowledge. The closer we come to equality for women, the smaller the gap between women and men's cultural experiences and thus their identity. That does not negate the need for transgender men and women to find gender harmony for themselves at a deeper place than social norms can touch.

All of the issues associated with our sexual preferences and identity are complex. As we sort them out, we are expanding the range of our acceptance and understanding of one another and ourselves as we confront centuries of prejudice and open windows on freedom.

As I close this section, the Supreme Court of the United States has declared same sex marriage legal and the law of the land. This decision came as a welcome and joyful surprise to many and a swift enactment of justice and confirmation of the rights embedded in the Constitution of the United States. There has already been resistance. Nonetheless, a fog of injustice has lifted and marriage is an institution that now takes on a new face of equality for all!

*****

Perhaps the most important thing to note after legal rights and protections have been won for those who have faced discrimination of any kind, is that we are whole people. Our sexual orientation along with our race or gender or ethnicity or physical ability or age does not need to define us, it is one part of who we are.

We are all on a spectrum related to sexual orientation and identity, on a bell shaped curve. We are all on a spectrum of color since many of us are of mixed race. The same could be said of ethnicity and nationality. Where we fall on the spectrum affects our socialization and experience in culture. And to be fair, so does our class, the way we are parented, our personalities, our physical condition, our age, and our education. Many different factors help define us and shape our identity and views. We can both accept and celebrate our differences even as we acknowledge the common humanity that binds us together.

We can stop thinking in polarizing dualities and accept the reality of complexity and embrace its beauty which, when embraced is elegantly simple.

People of Faith
FOR ERA

LOVE
CAREFULLY!
PLANNED
PARENTHOOD

EQUAL
PARTNERSHIP
IN
MARRIAGE

UNITED NATIONS
1975
INTERNATIONAL WOMEN'S YEAR

we try harder
and get
paid less

WOMEN
N.O.W.

THE WOMEN'S MOVEMENT AND FEMINISM

T HE WOMEN'S MOVEMENT was and is, so central to my thought and theology that I am surprised by how few buttons I have to reflect that reality. I have reams of papers, reports, and books on feminism. But few buttons. Nonetheless, the buttons I do have tell important parts of the story as I knew it.

My direct involvement with the Women's Movement began in 1968, when, as Director for Women's Program in the Board of Christian Education for the national United Presbyterian Church and Secretary for United Presbyterian Women, I inherited the work of a national women's advocacy group and The Task Force on Women was born. Working with a group of talented women, we began the exciting work of defining a feminist agenda in the Presbyterian Church.

Each year the Task Force would report to the General Assembly and a record of our work is in their official minutes. The first time we reported, the Assembly broke into laughter at the very thought of the existence of a task force on women. By the following year, they had stopped laughing. And their laughter had turned some women who had been observing into activists.

As we addressed issues, the Task Force worked hard together as a team. Elder Elaine Homrighouse was our first Chair. Task Forces were springing up across the country and groups of United Presbyterian Women were discussing women's causes. I personally visited groups of energized women in almost every state. Women were on the move and being effective.

In the course of our work, we joined with other church and secular groups committed to opening doors for women and freeing both women and men from the limitations of sexism.

Among the groups we worked with was The National Organization for Women, NOW. Their third Vice-President who served for two terms, Wilma Scott Heide, and I formed a lasting friendship as we worked together to define life beyond patriarchy. I also worked with Joyce Slayton Mitchell, another life time friend, as we initiated a Task Force on Religion in NOW.

The buttons you see signify years of exhilarating and productive work on the part of thousands of organizations and millions of women. They also represent sacrifice and struggle.

The buttons that follow represent only some of the issues that we addressed. During the time that we were addressing specific issues, we were also identifying theological, psychological, and philosophical issues, the values essential to the fullness of human development beyond the limitations and stereotypes of sexism. We addressed issues of power and peace, of separating religion from patriarchy and nationalism, of relational justice in intimacy, to name a few. These are things that are too complex for buttons. There is simple justice and complex justice. The search for new ways of being and relating continue. So does the need to address particular issues of simple justice. Simple does not mean easy to achieve!

We begin with **the ERA** button. This button does not refer to the popular laundry detergent. It refers to the Equal Rights Amendment that would be an Amendment to the Constitution of the United States. This Amendment was first proposed by Alice Paul in 1923 and finally passed by Congress in March of 1972. Feminists of all ilks found passing this amendment a matter of simple justice.

Everyone involved in the Women's Movement supported the Equal Rights Amendment and actively advocated for it, including women at all levels of religious life across the nation.

While women and men, secular and religious, worked hard for gender equality, achieving many of our objectives, we did not win the passage of the ERA.

The Amendment reads: Section 1. Equality of rights under the law shall not be denied or abridged by the United States or by any state on account of sex. Section 2. The Congress shall have the power to enforce, by appropriate legislation, the provisions of this article. Section 3. This Amendment shall take affect two years after the date of ratification.

After passing both houses of Congress it was passed on to the states for ratification during the next five years.

In the end the Equal Rights Amendment failed to pass by the required three fourths majority of states. The states that did not ratify were Alabama, Arizona, Arkansas, Florida, Illinois, Louisiana, Mississippi, Missouri, Nevada, North Carolina, Oklahoma, South Carolina, Utah, and Virginia. It would have passed if only three of these states had voted for it.

Looking back, the 19th Amendment to the Constitution which gave women the right to vote was not passed until August 26, 1920, after 72 long years of struggle. The more slowly an issue moves through channels, the more significant and structural are the changes it represents. The ERA is so significant that it didn't pass through those channels at all!

I was not sure that the Equal Rights Amendment would ever again be before us for ratification until I discovered a renewed effort to get it passed. We cannot avoid the issues. While women and men are experiencing more equality in American society than ever before, there is still much work to do. Our patriarchal super culture has cracks in it but it has not been replaced. We still need the Equal Rights Amendment in our Constitution.

President Barack Obama pointed out in 2014, that the inequality of pay between women and men is an embarrassment and a clear indication of our unfinished agendas.

Put the **We Try Harder and Get Paid Less** button and the **ERA** button together with the **Littlest Women's Symbol** button, and you get to the basics in women's long journey toward justice.

The Littlest button and most generic symbolizes equality for women. This particular button is old but it is still relevant for women of all races and classes and ethnicities, of all sexual orientations, and marital states, in countries all over the world.

The majority of the poorest people in the United States and the world are still women and their dependent children. Women need to be economically enfranchised and to achieve this we need to address the climate for women and work in the public sector as well as women and men's roles in the home, and their images in religion and culture.

It seems like a small thing, but it is symbolic. One of the early issues we addressed in our Presbyterian Task Force on Women, was the need for women to be known by their own names, Jane Smith, not Mrs. John Smith.

Traditionally, women serving on church boards and recorded on membership rolls, had been known by their husband's names. Of course, a few women had always been known by their own names for a variety of reasons.

Some women were indignant at the idea of change. They were proud to be, wanted to be called, by their husband's names. For the most part, that is different now. Most women want to be known for and as themselves, however much they respect and love their spouses.

The truth is that no matter how much a married woman values her relationship with her spouse, most women cannot count on being economically dependent on a partner for all of their lives. In order to escape poverty, women need economic equality and the ability to earn their own income and have their own identity. This is true worldwide. Simone De Beauvoir asserted this in her classic, **"The Second Sex,"** written in 1949.

*****

During the active years of the Women's Movement, women came together in conferences and informal gatherings to discuss sexism across the nation and in international settings. As we shared our experiences along with our dreams for the future, it became clear that women are second class citizens around the world. We needed to redefine our place in society and claim enfranchisement on all levels of our lives. We needed to do that in the context of our own cultures and sub-cultures. And we needed to be one another's advocates.

This came home to me one year when I attended a Conference on sexism in Mexico. Participants came from south, central, and north America. At the beginning of the Conference African American and Latina women spoke passionately and clearly about their struggles as women of color. Anglo women were silent. We had trouble finding our voice.

I think it was because we perceived ourselves as coming from a privileged class, race, and nation. We felt we were not supposed to have problems of our own. It was painful and hard to break our own silence. We were most at ease being advocates for others and that was what was expected of us.

Finally, when we talked, we talked about how hard it is for those of us who are married to have identities that are separate from our husband's and remain in loving and supportive relationships. We were not all married. Among us were lesbian women who were not free to be out in the church. All of us were white and mostly middle class women who had been the backbone of the patriarchal system, sticking to our roles and images, being good wives and mothers or proper single women. For many of us, dependence on men was a deep economic and psychological problem. We were taught to be ladies. We had to learn to relate to men as equals, accept our sexuality, and claim a place and authority outside of the home.

We had been accused of being man hating feminists and that was far from the truth. I am sure that feminism did upset relationships with men for some of us. But it was not because feminists hated men, it was because our new desire for equality was hard for some men to take. In the church and in society, we wanted to work with men who, with us, had a vision of a new social order.

As we talked together, women from all parts of America and many segments of life, we knew that liberation would be different for each of us as we confronted different manifestations of sexist culture. We knew that we were in this together, we needed one another as advocates. And we knew that we would all need to advocate for an end to racism and other forms of discrimination as we addressed sexism. Rights are indivisible.

I came away from that Conference knowing that while women of all colors and conditions have some different and some common struggles, we are stronger together. We need to listen to one another and take each other's stories seriously. And we each need to take ourselves seriously.

This little button with the symbol for woman on it, calls us all to stand in solidarity with all women who need the opportunity to live full and safe lives. By the time I attended **The United Nation's International Women's Year in 1975** (see that button), again in Mexico, women from developing countries and developed countries were working with one another to draft objectives that included everyone's needs and recognized our diversity.

The Press tried to present women from developed countries and women from developing countries as being at odds. That was far from the truth. We all wanted to cooperate and were good negotiators and were able to insure the inclusion of everyone's needs as we worked to draft documents describing the elements of justice for women.

I do not want to leave my reflections on international women's issues without mentioning my long-time, close friendship with the Rev. Dr. Beatrice Melano Couch. Bea and I went to Seminary together and continued our friendship until her death several years ago. Bea, an Argentine was one of the first Liberation Theologians in Latin America, a difficult journey for a woman, and a married woman with children. We were sisters in spirit. In the early years of our Task Force, she was an affective ally. From my relationship with Bea and women from other countries, I learned that sometimes our compatible personalities are stronger than our differences, national and otherwise, though we benefitted from learning about those differences.

Of course, equality is not just a matter of policy and law; it is a matter of public opinion and individual belief. Thoughtful feminists, both women and men, have long recognized that legal equality, while essential, is only part of the struggle. The women's movement is unique in that it addresses both social issues, sexuality, and intimate relationships between partners. In theory, some of us sleep with "the enemy." In reality, we sleep with human beings who are in need of liberation and wholeness even as we are.

And in my case, as a mother of three sons, I certainly could not say that I gave birth to "oppresors." That is ludicrous. As important as it was for me to work for equal rights for women and egalitarian relationships between women and men, it was just as important for me to let my sons know that I loved them for the men they were becoming. We were not engaged in a zero sum game. The more fulfilled women could be, the more fulfilled men could be. We could make society better together.

I respect those feminists who decided to focus solely on women and our rights in society. Women did indeed need to find their own voice and learn to be their own advocates. It took diverse perspectives and approaches to move feminism forward.

When the Women's Movement was past its heyday, the work of feminism continued and continues. We knew and still know that we need new ways of seeing and being both women and men and defining healthy relationships between people. From my perspective, from the family to halls of power, we need to step back from the battle of the sexes and move forward to productive and satisfying cooperation.

This does not mean that we do not address sexism and heterosexism head on as well. Women need to have the same opportunities as men and the same pay. We need to redefine roles in the family and understand that the best of so-called feminine and masculine characteristics belong to both women and men. And violence against women has to stop. We need to stand with women who have been violated and provide resources for their healing and strength. And violence within men's culture also needs to stop. We need to support men who conscientiously object to violations against men in male culture.

We fought and continue to struggle, long and hard as a nation, to prove that when it comes to race and ethnic origin, there is no such thing as separate but equal. When it comes to gender, there is no such thing as separate but equal either. I am not sure we believe that yet.

We have moved beyond those early stages of discernment. As women and men face issues of gender segregation in today's society, questions still emerge about biological determinism as we peel back the layers of sexist thought. We still have trouble accepting the fact that women and men are more alike than different. Our common humanity trumps our gender. I know that women and men do not come from different planets, though given our histories and conditioning, it sometimes seems that way.

I am aware that there are differences between women and men. I don't think they make much difference except in heterosexual sexual expression and giving birth. We simply need ways of reordering the images in our minds that shape how we see ourselves as women and men. Feminism can help demystify the feminine and masculine mystique!

In the first creation story in Genesis, women and men are both in the image of God. That says much about God and humanity. God is not one sex or the other, God is both and neither. God is One. And each of us human beings is whole in ourselves. None of us are anyone's other half.

As I look at my **ERA** button and **We Work Harder and Get Paid Less** button, I realize how many matters are tied up with and derive from equal rights for women. I am acutely conscious of the fact that, while we have made many gains in women's rights, we have not yet moved politically or religiously to a system of thought, social organization, and religious belief that thinks and functions beyond sexism and the gender segregation that supports it.

I know personally how challenging movement toward a new gender paradigm can be. Along with the difficulty of charting a new path, comes a new freedom. It is this that we celebrate and continue to work toward. As you can see from the next button, confronting sexism is about justice in all aspects of life from the public to the personal.

The next button says, "**Love Carefully**." Birth control has been a liberating force for women and not incidentally, men. Planned Parenthood, the organization behind this button, pioneered education and advocacy for the use of birth control and the education of people around issues of sexuality. Love carefully meant use and advocate for birth control.

As I write this," love carefully" means the same things it meant in my generation but with new twists. As a society, we can discuss sexuality more openly. We live in a much more liberated society than the one I was born into. We can engage in sex more freely. We can take birth control much more for granted. It is more accessible in more forms. The pendulum has swung.

However, as in my generation, unwanted pregnancy still exists along with unplanned pregnancy, and while we are more informed about sexually transmitted diseases, these diseases are still with us. The good news is that women are claiming their sexuality. The bad news is that in our society, women's sexuality continues to be exploited and cheapened.

The Women's Movement advocated caring for our bodies and owning them. It called for us to protect and enjoy ourselves emotionally and physically where sexuality is involved. We learned about female pleasure. We are still discovering new personal sexual liberation.

The Women's Movement also worked tirelessly to make safe abortions available in the face of unwanted and sometimes unsafe pregnancies. The availability of abortion did not make the ethical decision to have an abortion easy. It made choice possible for women and closed down unsafe abortion operations.

There are those today who are still working feverishly to take that choice away. The political work of protecting Choice and of keeping safe abortions available continues and is as important as ever. We must never again return to unsafe abortions behind closed doors.

We fought very hard against women's being seen as and treated as sexual objects. Women are complete people. We fought to bring the issue of violence against women to the fore.

In spite of more openness and awareness regarding our sexuality, we are living in a time when sexual violence against girls and women continues as does the struggle against it. Rape in the military and on college campuses is in the news. We are talking about it. Is it also on the rise? The sex trade is flourishing. And sexual violence in the home, including incest, remains a devastating problem. Hopefully, having these issues out in the open will enable us to address them with more determination and effectiveness.

Violence against women conflates sex and power and is one of the most heinous expressions of sexism. The Internet opens up ever more avenues for exploitation. We are just beginning to address internet avenues of abuse.

Loving carefully needs to be accompanied by the right to be carefully loved.

Now new questions come. Has the sexual pendulum swung too far? Is there a correction needed? Is women's sexual freedom being exploited? How do we want to define sexual ethics, not just for young people but for people of all ages both married and single.

Watching some TV shows and becoming aware of sexually explicit videos on the Internet, I get the impression that being sexually active and sometimes promiscuous, is being promoted as critical to being alive. Anything goes. Not having sex for weeks, months, never mind years, could be bad for one's health and psyche and social standing.

However wonderful sexual activity is, we do not die without it. And pleasure cannot be measured in quantity, the number of sexual encounters we have. Quality matters. Relational ethics matter. The need for deepening intimacy exists.

Our sexual organs are connected to our brains, our hearts, our spirits. When we engage sexually, all of us comes along. Making this connection may be key to our evolving sexual ethics.

There are many twists on what it means to "love carefully."

I look at the button again. "Love Carefully." It still applies. It is not just about birth control anymore. It is about valuing and using our sexuality joyfully, refusing to accept sexual objectification, wanting to be loved carefully.

Our human sexuality is available to us for pleasure and enhanced intimacy, and if we choose, procreation. It is a deep source of love between people. Loving mindfully, loving fully, and loving consensually go together with loving carefully.

*****

From loving carefully we move to loving justly and this shifts our attention to the button that says "**Equal Partnership in Marriage**." Marriage is a covenant and a legal agreement between two people who make a home together over time. It was once an institution that defined women as property, contributing to the oppression of women by the laws governing marriage. While marriage laws vary by state, married women were, universally, for a long time, considered under men's authority who were head of the household. Husbands were even free to physically discipline wives.

Married women are no longer considered property, we can own property, we have a right to be protected from domestic abuse, to obtain credit in our own name, to negotiate the place of domicile, and to keep our own names. And physical discipline is now called abuse. These rights have been won over time.

Women's unequal partnership in marriage was reinforced in the workplace by limited job options for women and unequal pay. Women were not supposed to work for pay because they were housekeepers and mothers with singular responsibility for the care of children and other sick or frail family members. When married women did work, it was to supplement their husband's income.

Our society had so romanticized marriage that we had protected ourselves from overt consciousness of the institutionalized inequality inherent in marriage. By my mother's generation, women did not, for the most part, work outside of the home. But they had gained more power in the home and for many, more respect in marriage.

Until Betty Friedan wrote **The Feminine Mystique** in 1963, there was not much awareness that this arrangement was a problem. Marital relationships were often solid, and functional, some very loving. One partner cared for children while the other provided financially. The problem was that equality for women cannot be achieved where this is the only norm, no matter how loving a marriage is. And women were not fulfilled. Patriarchy had defined not only our public institutions but the private institution of marriage. It also made it extremely hard for most single women with children to survive economically.

In my book "**Work after Patriarchy: A Pastoral Perspective**, (Xlibris in 2009), I write about finding a new paradigm for sharing work in the family, work for pay, housework, parenting, volunteer work. I see this as a key to individual wholeness and equality in marriage. Changing roles in the family requires shifting images and ideals that have helped define those roles by gender.

My work book was a hard book to write because its concepts were hard to live by. They still are but it is getting easier. What started out as a book about women and work, ended up being a book about both women and men.

I knew that women and men's lives need to change together. I came to the realization that when we try to shift universal cultural assumptions about gender that are etched in our psyches, we are dealing with powerful images affecting both sexes. These images and ideals have roots in both religious and secular world views that affect us all.

I had to confront those images and ideals in my own psyche. Only then could I speak of them with others. I had to confront gender segregation and ideas about "women's world" and "men's world." I was straddling both.

I am amazed at how far we have come in moving toward equality in marriage given our past history. I see that some of this change has come from economic forces that have made women's working for pay essential. Some of the change has come about by pursuing equality between women and men in marriage, and by acceptance of same-sex marriage.

As a clergy person, when I counsel a couple before marriage, I encourage them to think about how they plan to divide work between them and how they imagine their roles in relationship. There are no more easy assumptions. Unless there is disability or serious illness, most couples envision a fair division of labor based on their personal preferences, talents, and desires. That still takes conscious effort in the Twenty-First Century. Some couples choose roles that seem more traditional. What is important is that they have options.

We are witnessing dramatic changes in divorce laws along with changes in marriage laws. In some states, the equal division of property between divorcing couples is written into law. And over time, men have gained more access to the care of children as attitudes and practices about custody rights change. Parenting rights and responsibilities are increasingly shared between parents in joint custody settlements.

Most importantly, the thought behind this button "**Equality in Marriage**" continues to bring about more just relationships in marriage. That inevitably will make life more just in the public sphere.

This button reminds me that marriage is both about romance and reality. When I was in graduate school, I fell in love with and married a classmate, Thomas Fitch Kepler. Reading over some of my correspondence with him during times when we were apart, I am struck by my total absorption into the traditional role of wife and later, mother-to-be. I did not see being totally devoted to him, supporting him in his career and giving up my own as a sacrifice or problem. I was in love with love, the highest of callings!

I had to learn more about who I am and that love thrives best when I can be myself and relate to someone else being themselves. I found I enjoy cooperation and am good at compromise in most things. Living each day by grace and not taking everything too seriously helps.

*****

I look back on my mother and father's lives. They lived out the traditional paradigm. In spite of it, they were each amazing people. The human spirit can thrive even within unjust systems that need to change. So can love. I learned important lessons from each of them. I didn't need to repeat either of their lives or the structure of their marriage. The gift feminism gave me was the ability to incorporate both of their experiences in my life. With that change came many personal adjustments and ultimately much reconfiguring of relationships. It was hard work.

Equality in marriage, a critical key to ending sexism, takes work. There are no simple functional roles to fall into. And with both partners often working, time management becomes a challenge. But then, living together in intimate loving relationships has always required effort on the way to reaping its rewards.

Of course, many people are single heads-of-households. I was in that position for two years when our sons were teen-agers, and it was challenging. Seeing each partner in marriage as a whole person can and does contribute to our understanding that single people are not partial-people waiting to get married. It is all right to be single if that is our choice or our circumstance.

Now, years after the Women's Movement was in its heyday, a new wave of feminists will help to carry us forward. They will address the unfinished business of the past and forge their own agendas. They will have to struggle with complexity even as we did. I hope they benefit from the achievements of their forebears.

The last button on this page may be puzzling. **A 76 with a women's symbol and the letters WCTC**. The Women's Coalition for the Third Century was a Bicentennial organization that emerged out of a meeting of leaders of women's groups from all sectors of society called by President Richard Nixon in preparation for our national celebration and carried on by President Gerald Ford.

The button was designed by my sister Mary's husband, Bill Bradshaw, a commercial artist. This button deserves a section of its own.

THE WOMEN'S COALITION FOR THE THIRD CENTURY

"THE WOMEN'S COALITION is constituted to promote the empowerment and active participation of women from all classes, races and creeds as creators and leaders in all dimensions of the American Bicentennial celebration, and to work in concert with others concerned for the liberation of all people; to unify the women of this country through the celebration of the bicentennial era; to recover women's history, to celebrate women's contributions to culture; to build toward a fully representative democracy, and to create the future by moving beyond independence toward a more humane society based on interdependence." From the Minutes of the founding meeting in 1973.

I remember well the meeting that eventually led to the formation of The Coalition. President Nixon called women leaders together in November of 1972 to prepare for our nation's Bicentennial. Under the sponsorship of the ARBC (American Revolution Bicentennial Commission) we came to Washington

DC. We were seated around a large table, women from all segments of our national life: religious leaders, political leaders, university presidents, social activists. I was invited as a leader in women's work in the United Presbyterian Church.

We were exploring ways women could participate in the Bicentennial. As that and subsequent meetings wore on, some of us began to feel that we were being asked to play an auxiliary role in the celebration. We wanted to find ways to take a leadership role. While honoring the past and building on it, we were committed to contributing to the future directions our nation would take. We decided to form a group that would be independent of the ARBC and the Women's Coalition for the Third Century (1976-2076) was born, WC3C.

We developed our own structure and non-profit status, wrote our own by-laws, and elected officers as we began the Coalition's work. We set up committees to address women's contributions to our nation's history, and we decided to draft a Declaration of Interdependence.

The groups that signed the founding documents and continued to do the work of WC3C were: Federally Employed Women, the Leadership Conference of Women Religious, the National Coalition of American Nuns, the National Organization of Women, the National Women's Political Caucus, The United Presbyterian Church, USA, Women's Council and Church Employed Women, Women's Equity Action League, Women's International League for Peace and Freedom. Working with us were the Interstate Commissions on the Status of Women, the Intercollegiate Association of University Women, the National Black Feminists, and the United Methodist Church Women's Division.

Each of these organizations represented thousands of women and most had local chapters. Reading over the minutes from our meetings during the years leading up to 1976 is revealing and exhilarating. So many people were involved. So many programs took place all over the United States. We did indeed celebrate women's contributions to our nation over its first two-hundred years. And we advocated with one voice for opportunities for ever greater contributions in the years to come. We even endorsed a game on Women's History. The records of the Coalition now reside in the archives of the Schlesinger Library in Cambridge, Massachusetts. Their Librarian at the time, Patricia King, was on our Board.

Wilma Scott Heide from NOW was elected Vice-President, Edith Tebo, from Federally Employed Women was our Recorder, Sister Concilia Moran of the Leadership Conference of Women Religious was Treasurer, Dr. Linda DePauw, a professor and author from George Washington University was our Historian, Jean King was our legal advisor, and I, from the Presbyterian Church, was the President. Taffy Tarbell, also from the Presbyterian Church, was our primary staff person. Cathy Hall, a dear friend with whom I had worked in Presbyterian circles was an essential member of our network. We were all volunteers.

As we were developing a grass roots community, and connecting with programs across the country, we began to write the "Declaration of Interdependence" eventually accompanied by a Declaration of Women's Imperatives.

On the large button at the beginning of this section, you see men signing the Declaration of Independence in 1776. In 1876, one hundred years after that Declaration, women still did not have the right to vote. African American men had gained the right to vote in 1870. So, in Seneca Falls, New York, Elizabeth Cady Stanton and Lucretia Mott convened a group of women to draft a Declaration of Women's Rights. They stated that they were drafting their Declaration for women one hundred years hence in 1976. It would not be until 1920 that the 19th Amendment was passed granting women the right to vote.

In 1976, being the heirs of both documents and descendants of our forebears of 1876, it was time for us to speak and fulfill the mandate of our time. We were drafting a document on Interdependence on behalf of and for all Americans. Looking forward to our nation's Third Century, 1976-2076, we put our commitments and dreams in writing.

As we were drafting the Declaration of Interdependence, some among us called attention to the fact that while we were envisioning a time when cooperation and partnership between all of the peoples in the United States could become reality, we were still living in a time when women's rights were not yet secure. That led to the development of our Declaration of Imperatives as an essential part of and condition for equal partnership and interdependence.

As women, we would address our own rights, and we would go beyond that to work together with men toward a just, compassionate, and peaceful society. Some men contributed to the process.

The Preamble to the Declaration reads:

"Two hundred years ago the United States of America was born of the courage and strength of women and men who while searching for liberty, gold, or adventure, endured to lay the foundation of our nation with their lives.

Believing in a people's right to govern themselves, they drafted a Declaration, initiated a revolution and established this republic. Some who struggled for freedom were not fully free themselves: youth, native Americans, blacks, women of all races, and the unpropertied.

Each of us emerges out of the past with a different story to tell. We inherit a nation which has broken through to a technological age with the dangers and promises that holds. Responsibility rests on us. We are committed to the Constitution of the United States, augmented by the Equal Rights Amendment, and the evolving democracy it protects. We believe in the right of all people to self government.

History teaches us that unlimited power and powerlessness breed corruption, that where all human beings are not valued, humanity is violated, that where differences divide us, they limit and distort us; that independence is an illusion, and unlimited freedom is tyranny, plunging whole societies and people into chaos and bondage. Human survival requires interdependence.

We have been called to new consciousness by impending crises that threaten to overwhelm us if we obediently serve institutions that do not serve us.

We will no longer endure the corruption of power which risks the world's future by ignoring the well-being of persons and communities. The imperative of the present is to integrate the struggles for greater humanization, to be committed to the growth of one another, to develop and vitalize human community. It is necessary then to risk, to be in conflict, to suffer, to live, and to celebrate."

The Declaration goes on to expand on our interdependence, "With the Good Earth, "With All People, and "With Divine Reality."

The Declaration of Imperatives lays out the equality we intend to have as women who share responsibility for the creation of an interdependent world. It ends with these words:

"We will share the leadership of society and its government. We will demand respect for work inside and outside the home. We will share in the labor force and treasure leisure. We demand education that maximizes human potential. We will share in raising families. We will develop philosophies and theologies. We will enjoy our sexuality. We will create the future and act with strength in the fulfillment of these imperatives."

The full texts of these documents are in the Appendix.

The process by which the Declarations were finalized was truly democratic. An amazing number of people were invited to participate. We collected comments on an early version of the document from around the country. We had many executive committee meetings to refine it, and finally, at a meeting held at Emmanuel College in Boston in 1976, we voted on the final draft.

In many ways, without being naïve about women's place in society, we were ready to take steps beyond the struggle for those rights to claim a leadership role in moving our nation toward the future. The stereotypes that had dehumanized women had also dehumanized men and provided a model for other forms of discrimination. Gender issues stood alongside of other liberation issues as critical to movement toward a more just society. Justice issues were joined.

The Coalition represented a great diversity of women in the United States. As we drafted our Declaration, we were concerned that the rights of all be assured and that the future be built on principles and actions capable of sustaining all life for the future. I invite you to read the documents and as you do, think of the thousands upon thousands of women from very diverse backgrounds agreeing on what it says. Controversial issues were negotiated with great care and without compromising any groups' or person's integrity. That is the amazing reality undergirding our Declarations.

Looking back over the years when we met as a Coalition, I remember gatherings in our home, meetings in the Mother House of the Sisters of Mercy, conversations in government offices and educational and religious institutions. So many meetings. And many forums and activities. My sons, and some Harvard Divinity School students were involved in a special way.

For the big Bicentennial meeting of the Coalition where we officially adopted the Declarations, we put on a play, "**Eve and Adam and the Curse**," performed at Emmanuel College in Boston. Rehearsals for that play took place at Harvard Divinity School.

Our son, Tom wrote the rock music, Doug and Betsy Ruffle wrote the folk music, and I wrote the lyrics and directed the play about Eve and Adam, about the human race. Weeks before the play was to be produced, Tom came down with mononucleosis and could do very little but rest. The night of the dress rehearsal he left rest behind and performed with his band. His brother Jim, handled lighting and brother, John, worked on sound. The performance by Harvard Divinity students, went very well and received a standing ovation. The play was about interpreting the amazing Eve and Adam story in a new light for the healing of humanity.

On July 4, 1976, we held a signing of the Declaration of Interdependence, in Independence Hall in Philadelphia, where the 1776 Declaration was signed. That signing was followed by a service in the Unitarian Church where the 1886 Women's Declaration was celebrated. My good friend, Lynda Elliott, with her glorious strong voice provided inspiring music for both.

Before this official signing, we had gone to Washington and on the steps of the capital got signatures of several of the nineteen women serving in the House. Their names were on the official document: Millicent Fenwick, Shirley Chisholm, Patsy Mink, Bella Abzug, Patricia Shroeder, There were no women in the Senate in 1976. When the Bicentennial Celebration was all over, we presented the Declaration of Interdependence and its accompanying Declaration of Imperatives to the Smithsonian Institution for its historic collection.

We are now well into the 21st Century, we have entered our Third Century as a nation. The Declaration of Interdependence still speaks to us as does the Declaration of Imperatives. We did not achieve the passage of the Equal Rights Amendment that this Document assumes. We must now say that we are committed to our Constitution and the equal rights of women it must protect, leaving out the part about the ERA. The validity of the whole Document still stands.

As a society we are evolving toward interdependence at the same time that many forms of violence and short-sighted partisanship are tearing us apart. We need a way to bring together all of the forces for justice that defined the latter half of the Twentieth Century. Only then can we enable our nation, still young among nations, to be the democracy we are meant to be, and make a strong moral contribution to humanity's future. As a nation we are gifted with diversity and must pursue equality through cooperation.

It should come as no surprise that The Women's Coalition got no press in its time. We put out endless press releases. We had women in our coalition who were media savvy. But we were not controversial or disruptive enough to make the news. And though we were leaders in our time, we did not have enough sensational power to woo the press.

And yet, our work remains a part of history. Perhaps someday, that which was invisible in 1976 will become visible. Certainly, the ideas represented by the Coalition will live on and find their way into the social and moral fabric of our nation.

UMass
Here for a reason.

EDUCATION

THE BUTTONS ON this page represent the importance of education in all of our lives. They come from institutions of higher education, Drexel, Yale, Tufts, Harvard, The University of Massachusetts. If I had buttons for them, I would include Brandeis, Virginia Tech, Southern Maine Community College, University of Southern Maine, Roxbury Community College, the University of Montana West, Smith. These are all schools that have been or are, part of our family's lives.

I would also include buttons from elementary and high schools if I had them.

Whether or not we go to college, we all attend schools that educate us up to and through 12th grade or up to the age of sixteen. Many start their educational adventures in day care centers and nursery schools.

I think about my education. I went to Henry C. Lea public school in West Philadelphia for elementary school. I began in first grade as we did not have kindergarten then. I had to be dragged away from the arms of my mother on my first day of school! From Lea School it was on to Philadelphia High School for Girls in the center of the city. No buttons, but many memories.

Where there are students, there have to be teachers, administrators, and all the staff who make our school systems run. I am grateful to all those who contributed to my education and to those who have and continue to contribute to the education of all. Public education at all levels, right up through college is the backbone of our nation.

I have a special affinity for education because it has been, what you might call a family business.

My husband, Thomas Kepler's first parish was in Englishtown, New Jersey. When he went to his first Session meeting, there, to his surprise, was Charles Swalm, church elder, and Superintendent of Schools...and my first cousin! No escaping the family enterprise!

My aunts and cousins and sisters, my nephews and nieces, have all been teachers. My Aunt Mary, my father's sister, was the first in our family to get any education beyond high school. She went to Normal School (Teacher's College in those days) and began teaching in a one room school house that still stands out in the Pennsylvania cornfields. I think her daughter, Betty, who followed in her footsteps taught everyone in that Valley. Cousin Mary Schieb did too.

Our father was the first in his family to attend a four year college. He went on to get graduate degrees and then became a professor himself at Drexel. I can honestly say he was the best and most dynamic teacher I ever had.

Daddy was also Director of Athletics. When I was a child, Mary and I got to go to Drexel football games. Our family followed the team to surrounding colleges and explored campuses with my mother and sister, Mary, while he worked. Those experience really enriched my childhood.

Mother, who walked around college campuses with my sister and me while our team played, never went to college. She immigrated to the States alone at the age of sixteen and had to fend for herself. She did not have the opportunity to go to college though she helped put my father through school.

Living with my mother, I learned about innate intelligence. My mother had wisdom and knowledge that comes from life experience and personal fortitude.

While not everyone in my family went to college, in Tom's family everyone did. In his family, generations of the Blain/Keplers were clergy and missionaries in China. His mother, Margaret Blain, went to Wellesley and then to New York for Biblical studies. His aunt, Mary Tooker, studied medicine and became a doctor in the 1890s.

I got my college education at Drexel Institute of Technology, now Drexel University, along with my two sisters, brother, two cousins, and a brother-in-law. My husband got his college degree from Yale.

When I first took my husband-to-be to visit Drexel, he remarked, "This place looks like a High School." I suppose from a Yale perspective it did. I married him anyway. Drexel is now Drexel University with graduate and professional schools and an excellent educational rating. He would not be able to say that anymore. I brag about Drexel! He is proud of Yale.

I was the one who found the Yale button you see, in a way that surprised me. Nestled among the small towns and farms of central Pennsylvania is the farmer's market I have already written about. On one of our Friday visits to "The Sale," we stopped by a booth laden with all kinds of interesting objects including a basket full of buttons and pins. It was there, in that place, where the nearest institution of higher education is 45 minutes away that I found that Yale button. I thought it was a button for Yale locks. But, no, my husband assured me it was a genuine Yale item.

Tom and I, each coming from our individual experiences in education, both felt called to Ministry, which meant graduate school. We went to Princeton Theological Seminary where we both completed Master of Divinity degrees and Masters in Theology beyond that. And where, as they used to joke in those days, I got my MRS. Of course, that is sexist. I am Ms. just as Tom is Mr. Years later, I accepted a position at Harvard Divinity School as Director of Ministerial Studies.

I came by the Tufts button in another way. There I served as the Interim University Chaplain of the University... twice. I came out of retirement for my last term as Interim. It is a demanding job and my own ageism cast doubts in my mind about whether I should take on that job. Linda Karpowich, the Chaplaincy Coordinator believed in me. I should not have had any concerns with her on the staff. Her competence, knowledge, wisdom, and love for students, faculty, and staff alike had undergirded the work of several University Chaplains. We would be fine. Laura Manion another colleague contributed to the vitality of the office..

When our three sons were ready for college, I was Pastor of a local church and my husband was engaged in studies in Material Management. Like many others in the middle class, we had both too much money and not enough money to afford private colleges for them. They went to the University of Massachusetts in Boston. They were very independent young men and managed to work their way through school. They got a good education at UMass. One of them decided to go into the building trades half way through, rebuilding the South End. He has had his own construction business ever since then.

Our oldest son went on to get a doctorate at Brandeis where two of our daughters-in-law also earned doctorates. Over time, we have had connections to a variety of institutions of higher education. Think about the connections you have had and how the financial aspect of education was managed. We need to be aware of how families and many institutions of higher education struggle financially to insure an educated public able to keep the wheels of society turning and progressing.

While I hope all of our grandchildren finish college, I know that there are many forms of education and many self taught people who make the world go round.

Some of the most informed and discerning people I have known, were educated by life because they were paying attention. I have tutored parishioners who at the age of forty, could not read. Yet, they were good parents and wise citizens and able leaders in the church. I had two uncles who didn't go beyond eighth grade because they had to help their widowed mother, my grandmother, Mary Budd, raise a large family. Life provided their education.

From medical doctors and scientists, to artists and entertainers, to engineers and inventors, to social workers and legal advisors, to police and service personnel…the list can go on and on, all rely on one form of education or another to ply their trade. Education is at the heart of every life and all social systems. Educators should be at the top of our appreciation and pay ladder!

*****

Education is a lifelong adventure whether we are taking courses for credit, participating in continuing education for the sheer enjoyment of it, or expanding our horizons by exploring new places and subjects in our town or around the world.

I loved teaching in the Adult Education program at Tufts, OSHER. OSHER is a network of "Life Long Learning" opportunities for people over 50 with programs on many university campuses. It is our ongoing education that connects us to new people and communities helping to keep life vibrant and interesting.

Get out any buttons you may have and celebrate your education. Consider a positive vote for federal programs that make higher education a possibility for all through voting for politicians who care about those programs: that includes support for low interest student loans and more grants. And don't forget extra-curricular programs.

I think I learned as much in high school and college through participating in dramatic productions as I did through academics. I loved sports too. Music was my husband's passion.

Think about your education, formal and informal. And figure out what your next educational adventure will be. And while you are doing that, think about how we as a nation can provide excellence in education.

As I close this chapter, I muse about religious education. Education of our spirits and hearts is important to our well being. We spend five days a week for seven or eight hours a day, learning the three R's plus. Then we try to provide religious education for our children in an hour a week or less. It can't be done.

We rely on parents to bring their children up in faith if that is their choice, but often their own religious education did not go very far. As a nation we are fast becoming religiously illiterate.

Call me biased, but I think there is tremendous value in studying religion, especially the religion or religions that are our legacy. I would begin with our inherited religion because that is the one we will be best able to understand, absorb, and critique. Then we can branch out and study other religions, sometimes embrace them. Religion, of course, is about practice, experience, and faith as well as education.

There are those who choose not to embrace any religion. Even they might benefit from some religious literacy We can learn to honor one another's perspectives when it comes to matters of faith. That is not to say that we are not to be discerning about the effects of religious belief on our public life. It is to say that critiques, from both outside and inside of faith communities, need to come from informed minds and hopefully, open hearts, in order to be taken seriously.

*****

Education is for life. For all of life. What do your buttons (or thoughts about your education) tell you about who you are, what you have learned, and what you may yet need and want to know and discover. And who and what has helped shape who you are? I think this nation is what it is because of education. Democracy requires an educated public.

So, I close these reflections knowing that I value formal education and treasure it for all. And I value informal education, education on the road. And I value self knowledge. I value religious education. Much of what I have written about, civil and human rights, war and peace, feminism, celebrations of life, honoring the land, have been understood, worked for and embraced by people who have achieved various levels of education. They all have educated minds and spirits.

So, my ode to education, while an ode to formal education, is also an ode to the education that comes from noticing life, paying attention, being willing to mature, to grow up, to care about others along with ourselves, to be open to newness, to confront prejudice, to exercise good judgment, to respect ourselves, to honor the past on which we build, to consider the effect of our actions today on tomorrow.

I offer gratitude for teaching and learning in all forms. It significantly shapes who we are.

Celebrate our teachers. Celebrate students. (See our student appreciation button.) And celebrate the Spirit who confers wisdom.

THE BIG TIME IN A SMALL TOWN: THE STANLEY CUP

I F YOU LOOK at this button quickly, and are not a follower of ice hockey, you might think you are looking at a metal milk bottle. I did. I have a picture of my sister, Theresa touching the cup in admiration. In that picture, one can see it is a trophy, an impressive and hard won trophy. The Stanley Cup trophy to be exact. Above it is the name, Jay, and beneath it are the words, Williamstown (that would be, Williamstown, Pennsylvania). The date is 2004.

Jay refers to Jay Feaster, General Manager of the Bolts, the Tampa Bay Lightning, of the National Hockey League, winners of the Stanley Cup in 2004. Jay, it turns out, grew up in Williamstown, that small town I have talked about before, nestled in a valley that stands in the shadows of coal mountains in the Appalachian Range, north of Harrisburg, the state capital. In 2000, this town boasted around 1,300 people.

It was a surprise to find the Stanley Cup in this place. The Cup found its way to this small berg because members and managers of the team that wins the Cup in a given year can ask that the cup travel to a place of their choosing. In this case, Jay Feaster chose his home town.

The coming of the Stanley Cup to Williamstown was a very BIG deal. It deserved a parade. Tickets were given out to those who wanted to see it up close and touch it.

One lazy summer afternoon, members of my family were sitting on adjoining front porches of our homes that overlook the town's main street. As we were relaxing, we were surprised to see a crowd gathering in an area that is normally empty. We were curious about what was happening.

My sister, from Texas, and I were appointed to check it out. We went down to the street and walked the brief block up to the VFW Hall where the action was. In front of the milling crowd there was an open door. Interested, we went through it and up a flight of steps and there it was in all of its glory, the TROPHY. No one else was around.

We didn't realize it, but we had just crashed the lines, entered the building without a ticket, taken pictures of the cup, and left without being at all aware of what a violation of decorum our actions were. Our apologies to all those who had tickets and had been waiting in line!

Ignorance of the law, or of proper procedure, does not usually excuse one from wrong doing. However, in our case, innocence was bliss, and the people of Williamstown were not legalists or mean! People ignored, or maybe were unaware of our breach of the established rules of the day. But then, what does a Texan and New Englander know in Pennsylvania? I still feel a little sheepish about our adventure. But I learned some things about hockey.

Later, as we watched the parade celebrating the Bolts and Feaster, the significance of this day sunk in. A small town boy had made it into the big time and here we were sharing their big day.

Before that day, we had no idea what the Stanley Cup was, and, furthermore, we didn't have any idea about who Jay Feaster was. But the residents there knew.

Jay Feaster grew up in Williamstown and went on to become a lawyer. He worked for Herco, the Hershey Chocolate Company's entertainment arm, (made in the USA in PA) and in the process worked with the Bears, their hockey team.

Hershey, a town which we in Pennsylvania consider the chocolate capital of the world, lies about an hour south of Williamstown. In Hershey there is a world class amusement park with a classic roller coaster and almost all the rides one's heart could desire. (The only roller coaster I ever rode on…twice in a row, along with my cousin Betty who was a good sport enough to join me!)

From Herco, Feaster went on to finally become General Manager of the Bolts. Small town boy makes good. We had such a good time joining with all those in Williamstown who knew his story and were enthusiastically sharing in his success.

Actually, the parade that day was a double feature. Williamstown was honoring its veterans who had served overseas And I think it is fair to say that the Stanley Cup celebration, while it did not eclipse the veterans, certainly shared center stage with them. Sports really are important in America!

But, back to small town boy makes it in the big time. The reason we were all in Williamstown was that it was our father's home town. He also went on to become a lawyer and a professor of law. He too had an interest in athletics and was the Manager of Athletics at Drexel. He is, at least in our hearts, another Williamstown success story. No trophies, no Stanley cup, no parades, but from the perspective of our family and his students, he was our hero!

Where was that Stanley Cup years later? It just so happens that when I first began writing about this button, it was in the town where I live year round. The Bruins of Boston had won it. They had fought the Canucks of Canada in the play-offs for that coveted trophy.

I had never watched hockey in my life. Now I was glued to the TV set. We even watched one play-off game on a TV screen in a restaurant during dinner. At one point, a key Bruins player was pulled to the ground and injured. A collective gasp arose in the restaurant.

I found myself enjoying the fast paced game of ice hockey. The series that year stretched into seven games. When the Bruins finally won, what a victory! I always feel a little (sometimes a lot) sorry for the losers in any contest. The Canucks' disappointment was so palpable.

After that, the Stanley Cup began to make its rounds in the Boston area. We had a parade too. At one point, someone dropped the trophy, an important enough happening that it made headline news in the Boston Globe. I chuckle.

Sports can be such a unifying force in our communal lives. I know not everyone is into sports. And not everyone into sports is into all sports. Otherwise, I would have known what the Stanley Cup is. For those who enjoy sports, and for the many who take it seriously, it is like an art form. Skilled athletes performing at peak capacity. It is exciting, beautiful, and great entertainment.

And small towns can not only produce great men and women, they can be fun places to be when the big time comes home, this time through a sport's lens.

I know that people who live in small towns do not have to live small lives even if they do not move away and launch careers. The rest of my father's siblings stayed in Williamstown. They had full lives and were people I admired and loved deeply. In some ways, I got my early love of sports from them.

My uncle Dick and several cousins thought nothing of driving to Philadelphia to cheer the Phillies on, and the A's when Connie Mack's team was in Philadelphia. The Eagles were favorites too.

Later in our lives, John Erdman Kepler, my brother-in-law, was an avid Red Sox fan even though he lived outside of DC. Lucky for us, that meant trips to Boston and visits with him. Now his son Paul is taking up that gauntlet. He even ordered tickets for a game the day of his marriage to Jenny! Family fun!

I really like this Stanley Cup button. And now I can add ice hockey to the sports that I can enjoy… mostly. I will never be one of those people who know all the players and all the stats, though I did once know almost everything about the Phillies. (Now I am a Red Sox fan.) I am amazed at the swift and agile skating and strategic skill the athletes are capable of. The violent encounters that many fans love don't turn me on.

Jay Feaster remembered where he came from when he brought the Stanley Cup to Williamstown. We would all do well to remember our roots.

As a footnote, as a clergyperson I have upon occasion looked at filled sports arenas and fans' investment in winning and wished that people were as enthusiastic about attending religious services and as excited about them as they are about sports. But I have given those thoughts up. It will never happen and that's okay. Religion is not a diversion and while it can be playful, it is not play. Sports are play. Thank heaven for play! And for faith communities whose members are not spectators.

FIRST NIGHT

IN THE MIDST of all times and seasons, life rolls on, and with it, changing personal experiences along side of world events and shifting perspectives. I have seen many new years come and go. Some turning of time is remarkable and some is quite ordinary, as the months slip silently away. "A thousand ages in God's sight are but an evening gone." From an Einsteinian perspective, time is relative. Fleeting, relative, or seeming to stand still, time matters to us mortals. Our time on earth is measured in years. Time marks the seconds, the minutes, the hours, the years of our temporal existence.

One of the worst nightmares of my childhood was one in which time seemed to disappear and a sense of disorientation would take over. I would feel confused and frightened. Time orients us. So celebrating each new year is important to me.

The buttons I have that tell of New Year's celebrations, are those I have collected from First Night revels in Boston where we live. We have lived here for close to forty years and this is now home. These buttons mark the turning of time. They remind me of many new years that have come and gone and the other places we have been as the clocks chimed midnight.

*****

Since childhood, New Years' Eves have been magical for me.

Before my siblings and I were old enough to welcome in the new year, our parents, at the turning of midnight, would come upstairs and kiss us and say quietly, "Happy New Year."

Reaching the age when I was allowed to stay up until midnight on New Year's Eve was a big milestone in my life, a real rite of passage. Our family would count down the minutes to midnight, and then, on the (very late!) dot of the New Year's arrival, we would hug one another and take our pans and spoons and horns and stand outside in the cold night air and make noise. We would bang or blow on them happily along with our neighbors. When finally we went off to bed, we would sleep soundly having welcomed the first day of a new year.

In Philadelphia and its suburbs, where we lived until I was twenty, New Year's Day was marked by a Mummer's parade. Men in elaborate costumes marched and danced down the street, doing the Mummer's Strut to the tune of "O Them Golden Slippers." I still get a kick out of stretching my arms out as wide as they will go and doing that mummer's strut.

Nothing I did as an adult felt quite the same as the New Years' Eves of childhood.

The innocence and wonder of being young have a charm and warmth, when children are allowed to be children, that cannot be duplicated.

By the time my siblings and I were adults, we had scattered. We had our own network of friends and eventually, families of our own, and new traditions and celebrations.

When I became an adult, the outdoor-noise making with neighbors yielded to the indoor activity of watching television. Television added a new dimension to marking the New Year. Living in the Northeast, we could watch the huge crowd in New York ring in the year as a giant ball would descend after the seconds were counted down to midnight. That is, on the years that we were at home.

In the seventies, some artists in Boston got the idea of holding a special New Year's Eve celebration in our city with lights and performances, with ice sculptures, and fireworks. They imagined thousands having fun in the frosty December air.

We went to the first of these **First Night** celebrations in 1976, the year of our nation's Bicentennial. And in the years that followed, we enjoyed many more Boston First Nights, as the buttons show. On those years when we went to First Night we became part of a happy, enthusiastic, peaceful crowd, milling around in the cold. Motion everywhere, stimulating sights and sounds, and lights! Usually it was crisp and clear and we could see our breath. Only once do I remember snow.

As the years wore on, the crowds grew. One special First Night we headed into Boston with our good friends Judy and George Lambert, and JoAnne Beaman who was visiting from New Jersey. It was that one time that it was snowing and we were bundled up like Eskimos.

George, an Episcopal priest, was on the staff of St. Paul's Episcopal Cathedral, right in the center of the city. He got us in through the back door for a glorious musical performance that took place in their sanctuary. The crowds were now mushrooming and that usually meant waiting in long lines for events. We felt very special as we slipped in the back way. It was great. We knew the right person. It was one of the few times in my life that I have known someone who could get me in through the back door! I have to admit that I resent those who have and use entitlement as a life style. But occasional entitlement is great!

After the performance we ducked into a fast food place for some hot drinks. Judy and JoAnne are gone now and the good times we had with them are a treasured reminder of our friendships.

One memorable year, Tom and I spent First Night in a fancy hotel in Boston. Our sons were in their early twenties and wanted to have a New Year's party in our home. They offered to pay for Tom and me to stay in town. We happily agreed. We enjoyed that New Year's Eve almost as tourists, especially appreciating the ice sculptures on New Year's Day. They said their party was a huge success. The house survived and so did they, and we didn't ask too many questions.

There are many times in my life, when looking back, I have to ask, what was I thinking? All I can say is that they were young, and we were pretty young too.

There were also First Night celebrations in Boston spent with members of Clarendon Hill Church in one another's homes and in the city. I remember taking a subway ride into town one year to celebrate, parents and children all bundled up against the cold. The ride was part of the fun.

I can still see the fireworks as we stood on the banks of the Charles River in Cambridge, a group of happy church friends welcoming a new year.

Another time, we enjoyed a very special Middle Eastern New Year's Eve party with our friends. Great fellowship, food, and dancing.

One of these New Year Buttons marks The Millennial New Year and the changing of a Century. We welcomed in the year 2000 elaborately and excitedly with all kinds of special effects, from unique eye wear and hats to horns and champagne glasses. I, for one was delighted to be celebrating this marking of the turning of one hundred years…one thousand years! When I was a young woman, 2000 seemed so far away, like a time in science fiction.

In fact, the film, "2001: A Space Odyssey", seemed to be far in the future. Now, around the world, 2000 was really here! We were entering odyssey time!

Who would have thought in 1959 that in 1999, we would be worried that computers would crash because they could not calibrate the numbers. Computers were now a central part of our lives. Could technology handle the turning of time? Surely humans could and had for centuries. As it turned out, technology was up to the challenge. In fact, all was rather peaceful and ordinary that new year. The world kept right on spinning as a new century dawned.

One year, Tom and I took part in Raleigh, North Carolina's first First Night celebration. We were visiting our son Tom, wife Grace, and their children, Lenora and Kieran. The children were young so we could appreciate activities geared toward them. We made masks and all sorts of crafts in a huge cavern of a room. Then, heading home, we happily walked down the uncrowded middle of the road, humming and free. No crowds yet! The children's enthusiasm took me back to my own childhood.

Later, when they were older, there was a Japanese dinner in North Carolina with Lenora, our oldest granddaughter. And breakfast with her brother, Kieran, the next day.

*****

There were times sitting with son John and his wife Martha and daugthers Alana and April in their living room. And the times we were in Maine with our son Jim and wife Lisa and young Jim and Aly. There in the snow, we could welcome in another year under the beauty of the stars in the night sky, far away from bright city lights.

There was a special celebration with Lynda Elliott, our close friend with the expressive brilliant operatic voice, who was visiting from New York. I can hear her telling stories and laughing and lighting up the night as only she could as we ate Lasagna, her traditional New Year's dinner. And the time we spent with Carole and David Lawton, enjoying our neighbors and longtime friends and also gifted musicians.

Some new year's eves Tom and I had a quiet night alone, sipping wine and waiting for the birth of another year.

And, oh yes, there was the New Year's Eve before those evenings, spent at the Chapel in Logan Airport. Tom and I were separated, he was in Philadelphia and I was in Boston, but we wanted to spend some time together as a family. He flew into Boston and arrived just before midnight. I went to meet him and as we were walking down the corridor after he had deplaned, we came across the Chapel. We popped in for a moment as the hour was changing and said a little prayer. He finally moved to Boston and we reunited.

We have had many different kinds of New Year's celebrations that are not commemorated on buttons. I invite you to think of your own experiences as I think about some of ours.

The Buttons reminding me of first nights past carry many memories of the changing of time and times. They also remind me that all people don't celebrate the new year on January 1st. We have celebrated many lunar New Years with our friend Ching Ling Kung and her family. She became a Doctor in China and when she emigrated from China, she brought that tradition with her. We marked another Lunar New Year with our friend Betty Lin and her husband, Poping, in the California sun. I love having two new year's celebrations and two opportunities to declare a new beginning. The lunar New Year resonates with my husband Tom who grew up in China, settling finally in the States when he was fourteen.

*****

In Isabel Allende's memoir, I read a phrase that seems so right, "time went on behind our backs." Time can be like that. Before we know it, we are aware that we will someday experience some Last Night. So, as time "goes on behind our backs," time can provide us with a reminder to live in each moment, showing up for life, sloughing off worn out emotions, beliefs, parts of ourselves that have become outdated at best and toxic at worst.

Living in the present does not keep us from remembering the past or preparing for the future. Living in the present reminds us not to stay in the past, to pay attention to the now, having prepared as best we can for the future.

I think that celebrating the coming of each new year, while it calls for a recognition that time is marching on, nonetheless, provides us a time to just be, a night when time stands still…as in the moment, we live the last moments of the old year. Even as we count down time, midnight is a witching hour which stands between past and future.

In the morning, when a new year dawns, our attention can turn to New Year's resolutions. As the year begins, we are ready to work for, live for… a better us, a better world, better relationships. Go on a diet…exercise more…be kinder. We make promises to ourselves. Or not. And we go on. We live with the changes the old year brought. Sometimes there is someone new in our lives. Sometimes we have lost someone we have loved. Sometimes our health changes or our job. Whatever has been, we move forward.

Sooner or later, we get things in perspective. The future is, after all, only partially in our control. We are responsible for some things. Some things we have no control over. We know there are going to be surprises, some wonderful, some sad, some boring, some fascinating, some challenging. I go into each new year with a prayer on my lips. God go with me and those I love. And be with our wonderful and needy world.

We live in the context of one another's lives as well as in the context of our inner landscape. As years fold into years, we change, our relationships with one another change too, and our context changes.

As the world and the culture around us changes, we are affected. The question is, how aware are we of its influence and how do we affect it back? The choices we make or don't make have consequences.

In some ways, each of our birthdays marks the end of one personal year and the beginning of another. We celebrate those we love. We celebrate our own lives. Happy Birthday! May this be a great year!

In the midst of all of these first nights, eventually comes a first last night.

Dr. Harvey Zarren tells our heart group that when people are dying, facing their first last night, there are just four things that are important to say: Thank you; I forgive you; please forgive me; and I love you. These four things seem important to say and act on as each year turns, even when we are not at death's door.

Along with all of our secular celebrations of new years, religious traditions too have ritual times for marking the turning of time. Judaism has the Day of Atonement and Rosh Hashanah, and Islam has Ramadan and Eid. In Christianity, the new liturgical year begins with Advent, but in many ways, Lent and Easter mark a religious new beginning. Other faiths and cultures have special occasions and calendars for saying good-bye to the old, and welcoming new beginnings.

*****

January 1 marks a New Year in our Western secular calendar. I love its playfulness, the parties, the fireworks, and the quieter times with family and friends. And I have these buttons that allow me to remember things about First Nights. I deal with serious matters all the time. I worry about the state of the world and the health of my family and my own well being.

I enjoy New Year's Eve as a time when, even while time is being marked as moving on, time seems to stand still for one night of revelry or reflection, or both, until a new year breaks. I appreciate those times when our divisions and differences are set aside for a common night on the town.

May we all have many "first nights" of delight and promise: marking the turning of a year, a religious rite of passage, a personal first. We will have some first nights that surprise us and take hold of us unawares. We will have some ho-hum turnings in our lives and that has to be all right too. And on those first nights that are more somber and hard, because of loss or sickness, or separations, we continue on. We mark time through all seasons.

I admit as I think about these things, that while I recognize the distinction between secular and religious times of celebration, I see a holy Spirit breathing in all of life. I look again at the banner Sister Concilia made for me, "Sing to God a new song." So, as times unfurls before us, let it find us singing a new song along with the old ones.

APPENDIX

Declaration of Interdependence

Preamble

Two hundred years ago the United States of America was born of the courage and strength of women and men who while searching for liberty, gold or adventure, endured to lay the foundation of our nation with their lives.

Believing in a people's right to govern themselves, they drafted a Declaration, initiated a revolution and established this republic. Some who struggle for freedom were not fully free themselves: youth, native Americans, blacks, women of all races, and the unpropertied.

Each of us emerges out of the past with a different story to tell. We inherit a nation which has broken through to a technological age with all the dangers and promises that holds. Responsibility rests on us. We are committed to the Constitution of the United States, amended by the Equal Rights Amendment, and the evolving democracy it protects. We believe in the right of all peoples to self-government

History teaches us that both unlimited power and powerlessness breed corruption; that where all human beings are not valued, humanity is violated; that where differences divide us, they limit and distort us; that independence is an illusion and unlimited freedom is tyranny, plunging whole societies and people into chaos and bondage. Human survival requires interdependence.

We have been called to new consciousness by impending crises that threaten to overwhelm us if we obediently serve institutions that do not serve us.

We will no longer endure the corruption of power which risks the world's future by ignoring the rights and well-being of persons and communities. The imperative of the present is to integrate the struggle for greater humanization. To be more fully human is to share life, to respond to the dignity of ourselves and others, to be committed to the growth of one another, to develop and vitalize human community. It is necessary then to risk, to be in conflict, to suffer, to love and to celebrate.

We therefore make this declaration. We are interdependent with the good earth, with all people, and with divine reality.

In declaring our interdependence with all peoples, we recognize geographic communities of persons and their interdependence with one another. We affirm our common humanity and we respect one another's uniqueness. We accept our responsibility to share the visions, hopes and dreams of one another and pledge ourselves to protect each other's freedom.

We shall be dedicated to the empowerment of all people and to the expression of each person's creativity.

We shall commit ourselves to a world in which food, shelter, clothing and health care are the rights of all people.

We shall seek protection for people in need of care in our society, and work to provide support systems for those responsible for their care and nurture.

We shall create a climate for the creative development of each person's human potential, and for the utilization and enjoyment of all human resources for the good of all people.

We shall respect the dignity and privacy of expressions of individual personality and living relationships.

We shall be committed to lifelong learning with access to education for all persons and for the responsible uses of communication media.

We shall be committed to all people's responsibility for public institutions of government, law, education, business, and religion, and to the concept that those institutions be responsive to the direction of the people.

We shall value and share use of free access to all public information and shall protect and value individual privacy.

In declaring our interdependence with the Earth we affirm our reliance on it, our mutual responsibility for it and the rights of all persons to the fruits thereof.

We shall enjoy, protect, restore and improve the world that we inherit.

We shall produce the world's resources and share them among all peoples.

We shall enjoy and cherish the sacredness and privacy of our bodies and shall bring into the world children who are wanted.

We shall use and control technology for the survival and protection of nature and all people.

In declaring our interdependence with Divine Reality we recognize the possibilities of a sacred mystery within and around us.

We shall honor and protect people's right to gather as they choose in religious communities.

We shall support each other in pursuit of truths which emerge from our diverse experiences and histories, rejecting those exclusive claims to truth which deny the sacred existence of others.

We shall be open to revelations that extend beyond the boundaries of our current understanding and wisdom.

We shall recognize the divine within ourselves and in one another.

We women and men and children make this Declaration living in the midst of a world in which women can be subservient and oppressed, men can be repressed and brutalized, and children can be violated and alienated. In making this Declaration we seek a new order and covenant ourselves to a fully interdependent society. We live in a world in which love has often yielded to war, religion to materialism, and sexuality to violence. We are committed to the discovery of a humanity which lays claim to the fullness of life.

We disclaim any right to privilege in order to honor the full dignity and development of all and take up responsibility for instituting freedom.

We long for light to shine on our darkness and life on the shadow of death, and for our feet to be guided in the way of peace. We shall live with grace and struggle with courage through the transitional years that lie ahead.

The Women's Coalition for the Third Century offers this Declaration of Interdependence to the people of the United States for response. In so doing we declare our intent to be architects of our Third Century. The future belongs to those who can dream with courage and creativity, plan with intelligence and wisdom, and act with power and compassion for the liberation of humanity.

We invite others to join us in this declaration.

Declaration of Imperatives

We are aware of humanity's suffering, for as women we have been in bondage to unjust systems. Now we will define ourselves and find release from the values, images, myths, and practices that for centuries defined us.

We will no longer be governed by institutions that do not seek, respect and include our leadership.

We will not be taxed without representation.

We will not be bound by the authority of legal systems in which we participate only minimally in the making and administration of the laws.

We will not be exploited in the labor force.

We will not be the only ones responsible for child care, homemaking and community building.

We reject educational systems that distort our reality.

We will not accept philosophies and theologies that deny our existence.

We will not abide prophets of the future who ignore our struggle.

We will not be reduced to sex symbols nor have our sexuality determined by others.

We will not be the principal source of morality for this nation. We insist that our contributions to conscience be incorporated into the public as well as the private sector. And we will not be destroyed by unethical and immoral leadership. We will not be divided by the distinctions that have traditionally alienated us from one another.

We will share the leadership of society and its government. We will demand respect for work inside and outside the home. We will share in the labor force and treasure leisure. We demand education that maximizes human potential. We will share in raising families. We will develop philosophies and theologies. We will enjoy our sexuality. We will create the future and act with strength in the fulfillment of these imperatives.

The Women of the Coalition for the Third Century make this Declaration to make certain our rights are not once again denied and our value and values ignored. Our concern for interdependence requires of each full partnership with all in the search for a human order.

Printed in the United States
By Bookmasters